The North East Guide to Grants Organisations

Seventh Edition (2003 – 2004)

Researched by Linda Whitfield, FINE

Edited by Nicola Gray, Linda Whitfield, Tony Youll, FINE

<u>With contributions from:</u>

- Helen Attewell, The Community Fund

- Gillian Stacey, County Durham Foundation

- Fiona Ellis, The Northern Rock Foundation

- Peter Ellis, Lloyd TSB Foundation for England and Wales

- John Sharland, former Trust Secretary, Sir James Knott Trust

- Chris Blenkarn, Information Officer, One Voice Tees Valley

- Louise McGlen, Funding Adviser, Newcastle CVS

- Amanda Mockridge, former Liaison Officer, DAYCO

- Jen Wales, Funding Adviser, STRIDE

- Members of the Funding Advice Workers Network North East

Published by; Funding Information North East, John Haswell House, 8/9 Gladstone Terrace, Gateshead, NE8 4DY.
Tel: 0191 477 1253
Fax: 0191 477 1260
Email: enquiries@fine.org.uk

Printed by; Bakershaw Ltd, North Tyne Industrial Estate, Whitley Road, Longbenton, Tyne & Wear, NE12 9SZ
Tel: 0191 266 0409
Fax: 0191 270 1647
Email: enquiries@bakershawprint.co.uk

ISBN 0 9514754 6 0

Funding Information North East (FINE) gratefully acknowledges the financial support of the following trusts during 2001/2002

Barbour Trust

County Durham Foundation

Greggs Trust

Hadrian Trust

Joicey Trust

Sir James Knott Trust

Lloyds TSB Foundation for England and Wales

Northern Rock Foundation

The Rothley Trust

Sherburn House Charity

The 1989 Willan Charitable Trust

Registered Charity Number 510764 (GVOC)

CONTENTS

Introductory Section

Trust Details

CONTENTS (Cont..)

About The Guide

This is the 6th edition of the North East Guide for Grant Seekers.

It contains information about the grant-making policies and procedures of charitable trusts which support voluntary and community groups in the North East of England (Northumberland, Tyne & Wear, County Durham and Teesside).

Most trusts in this Guide have confirmed their entry, which is based on information contained in guidelines for applicants, annual reports and accounts. FINE is very grateful to all the trusts for their co-operation in compiling this Guide. Other entries are based on information received from the Charity Commission and previous information held by FINE.

The Guide contains information on Charitable Trusts which support the voluntary and community sector in the North East. Sources of funding available to the sector such as, the various National Lottery distributors, central and local government and Europe are not included in the Guide. If you require further information about these sources of money contact your Local Development Agency (LDAs). Contact details for the LDAs in the region can be found on pp12 – 13 of this guide.

FINE would particularly like to thank The Barbour Trust, Greggs Trust, County Durham Foundation and Sherburn House Charity for their generous donations towards the cost of researching and compiling this Guide.

Each edition of the Guide has been different and has continued to improve upon the work of previous compilers and hopefully this edition carries on that tradition. Please contact FINE if you have any comments or suggestions to improve future editions.

IMPORTANT

The Guide is published every two years. If you wish to be informed of any changes in the meantime, please complete the inserted page at the front of this Guide and return it to FINE. There is no extra charge for this service.

How To Use The Guide

The trusts are listed in alphabetical order.

If you already know which trust you want to read up about, use the Index on page 3 to find the page number for that trust's entry.

If you want to find out which trusts in the Guide fund your particular area of work (e.g. older people), use the Subject Index on pages 177 - 190.

Please read each entry very carefully to check that there is no obvious reason why you should not apply to a particular trust (e.g. your beneficiaries live outside the trust's geographical area of benefit). Pay particular attention to the Exclusions section, which lists what the trust will not fund.

Sending applications which show that the available information has not been read and absorbed only adds to the frustration of the trust's correspondent and increases the likelihood of your application going straight into the bin.

Carefully targeted applications, on the other hand, are welcomed by most trusts and usually have a reasonably high success rate.

Once you have identified trusts which look appropriate for your needs, you may wish to use the table of Meeting Dates on pages 22 - 25 to decide what order to approach them.

Before You Start To Fundraise

Before your organisation researches which trusts to apply to, it is important to bear in mind the following points:

The Fundraisers

Who is going to be responsible for the fundraising? Will it involve everyone or should you set up a special committee?

Raising money requires many different skills (e.g. written and verbal communication skills, enthusiasm, creativity, organisational abilities, confidence and commitment) and one of the first tasks should be to identify people within the organisation with such skills.

Similarly, you should identify any potentially helpful contacts your organisation already has (e.g. with local businesses, philanthropic organisations like the Rotary Club or the Women's Institute or Trustees of local trusts) to help directly or indirectly with raising funds.

Charitable Status

An organisation which is not a registered charity will find it more difficult to raise funds from trusts than an organisation which is registered. This is because the majority of trusts

are themselves registered charities and must therefore confine their grants to purposes which are charitable in law.

When a trust is asked to give a grant to an organisation which isn't a registered charity, it must take more care to satisfy itself that the purposes for which the money is intended are charitable. Some trusts will, if satisfied that your work is charitable, pay grants directly to non-registered charities.

If a trust specifies that it will only make grants to registered charities, you have two options:

- investigate whether your organisation could be registered as a charity and, if so, decide whether or not to get registered.

OR

- find a registered charity which is willing and able to accept the grant on your behalf, on the understanding that this intermediary charity passes the grant on to you.

The Charity Commission produce a very helpful pack called "Starting A Charity and Applying for Registration' which is available free of charge - see page 10 for contact details. Registering as a charity is a relatively simple process and is currently free of charge. The process usually takes 3 - 6 months.

Your local Council for Voluntary Service (CVS) or Rural Community Council (RCC) can give advice on registering as a charity and can also accept grants on behalf of non-registered charities - see pages 12 - 13 for contact details.

If the purposes of your organisation are not charitable at all, then there is no point in attempting to raise money from trusts.

Constitutions
Do you have a constitution which sets out the aims and objectives of the organisation and the rules governing how the organisation is managed and run? This reassures funders that you are a responsible organisation and is a necessity if you want to become a registered charity or apply for funding from e.g. the Community Fund. Your local CVS or RCC can give advice on how to draw up a constitution.

Bank Account
You should open a bank or building society account in the name of the organisation before you start to fundraise. For security reasons, it is a good idea to have at least three signatories and to ensure that two people are required to sign each cheque.

Letter Headed Paper
Does your stationery include a contact address and, if applicable, your charity registration number? Is it clear from your name what your organisation does? Your local CVS or RCC may be able to help you design and print stationery relatively cheaply.

Raising Money Yourselves
Most funders want to see that an organisation is trying to raise some of its funds by its own efforts, no matter how small a percentage of the total income this provides.

Organising a fundraising event is still one of the best ways of funding voluntary activity and can help to raise awareness of your organisation and its work. You could also consider charging for the services you provide to bring in additional funds

It is important to get as many different sources of income as possible so that you are not relying on any one source, which would leave you in a very vulnerable position when that source comes to an end.

Planning Ahead
Raising money takes time. Forward planning is essential and a clear fundraising plan is a good way of clarifying what you need to do and when, so that you are not constantly raising money for the short term.

Drawing Up A Budget
A budget is simply your group's plans in the coming year set out in money terms. Don't underestimate the time it will take to do the work needed to get accurate figures. Start work on the budget as soon as you can.

There are basic costs that nearly every group has, such as postage, stationery, rent, electricity and telephone bills. There may be other costs related to the work your group does, such as transport or catering. If you can find out the precise cost of something – do it! If you need to buy a piece of equipment, get quotes from a few different suppliers or use catalogues. Ask other similar groups how much they spend each year.

N.B. Don't forget to include expenses like training (for staff/volunteers / management committee members), National Insurance and pension contributions for paid staff, inflation in future years, volunteer expenses, VAT on goods / services, repairs, renewals, insurance etc.

Some funders will only make grants for capital costs (office equipment, buildings, etc), while others are prepared to fund revenue costs (salaries and other costs associated with running the organisation or project) Divide your budget up in this way, to help you decide which funder to approach for what.

Budgets aren't simply there to help your group raise funds - they are your guide to whether you are spending your money as planned. You should compare your expenditure to the budget every month or so, to keep on top of how much you're spending on what and to alert you early on that you may not have enough money later on in the year to do what you planned.

Accounts
Unless you are a new group, funders will ask to see your previous years accounts to reassure themselves that you are financially secure and can manage any funds they give you. All registered charities need to prepare annual accounts, although the rules differ depending on the size of income or expenditure.

Accounts can be prepared in different ways and may need to be independently examined or audited, depending on the size of your group. Your local CVS or RCC should be able to help you prepare accounts. Guidance publications are also available from the Charity Commission.

Keeping Records
You need a system for keeping records of who you have applied to, when you

applied and what the result was. For example, a trust may tell you that it doesn't have any money left this year, but you should re-apply next year. If you don't have a good system, you will probably forget! A system also means that if the person responsible for fundraising leaves, your organisation will know what they have done in the past.

Saying Thank You
If you do get a grant, remember to thank the funder and send them annual reports or press cuttings, showing them what you've done with the money and perhaps inviting them to come and see what you do. It is important to try and build up a good relationship with your funders.

Approaching Trusts For Support
A grant-making trust or foundation is a body set up to make grants for charitable purposes.

According to The Charities Aid Foundation, there are around 9,000 grant-making trusts in the UK, giving in total about £2.6 billion each year to charitable causes.

Usually, money (capital) is invested and the income from the investment is distributed in grants, although some trusts (e.g. BBC Children In Need, Comic Relief) raise funds themselves and make grants from the proceeds of their appeals.

Charitable trusts are diverse, independent and quirky. Some are secretive even furtive, some are innovative, some stick to an unchanging list of charities and others seek new projects and areas of interest to support. **It is therefore important to know as much as possible about the charitable trusts from which you are seeking support**.

In researching available information on charitable trusts, the following factors should be taken into account:

Objects
The character of a charitable trust is principally shaped by the legal document (trust deed) setting it up. In many cases, this is restrictive. Today many trusts are drawn up with wider objects so that they are capable of re-interpretation. Those with "general charitable purposes" can fund anything deemed to be charitable.

Policies
Charitable trusts usually formulate a policy to guide them in the spending of their income. Ask for the most up-to-date policy guidelines to be sent to you as they are helpful indicators of the type of grants made.

Income
The income of trusts varies enormously from several million to a few hundred pounds.

Geographical Area of Benefit
Many trusts are restricted to a particular geographical area. Trusts in this Guide have stated their area of giving.

Beneficiaries
The sort of people whom the trust was set up to benefit e.g. young people, single parents, people with disabilities.

Trustees
The Trustees of charitable trusts are a very mixed assortment of individuals. They can be peers of the realm, company directors, members of the Founders family, businessmen, churchmen etc. but they are all volunteers with a variety of charitable motivations. Bear all this in mind as it will affect their outlook and the projects they are likely to support. If you happen to know a Trustee of a trust, tell him or her that you are applying. In general, however, you should always deal with a trust through its designated secretary or correspondent.

Administrative Capacity
The larger trusts employ their own staff, but many of the smaller trusts may be run from someone's home or via an accountants or lawyers, so their administrative capacity is limited.

The sheer volume of applications, however, means that most do not normally acknowledge applications and many are unable to reply to applicants who are ultimately unsuccessful. If you want to be sure of an acknowledgement, send a SAE with your application

Size of Grant
What is the average size of grant the trust usually makes? Are grants made over a number of years?

Timing
How often and when, do the Trustees meet to consider applications? How long does it usually take to process applications?

Appropriateness

Is the work of your organisation appropriate to the work of the charitable trust? Many trusts, provided they have the capacity, welcome preliminary telephone calls as it helps them and the applicants, by reducing the number of ineligible applications. If a telephone is listed USE IT if you are unsure whether your project fits the funders criteria.

Armed with up-to-date information you can begin making your approaches.

Funding Information Sources

Charitable Trusts Themselves

Whilst some trusts continue to be secretive about their work, more and more information is available about trusts on a national basis. In general, trusts recognise that it is in their interests to provide accurate information about their policies if they wish to reduce the number of inappropriate applications they receive and continue to attract applications which interest them and fall within their guidelines.

Most trusts produce reports about their work and / or guidelines for applicants. Trusts also produce Annual Reports which give an annual picture of the trust's financial status as well as their previous year's grant-giving pattern. It is important to obtain as much information as possible about a trust before applying to ensure you make your application in the correct way.

The Charity Commission

The Charity Commission maintain a public Register of Charities on a computerised database which can be examined at any of their three offices (see below). The Register contains key particulars of all registered charities - the governing document, most up-to-date accounts (with details of grants made), the latest correspondent details etc.

Copies of extracts from the Register, and of governing documents and accounts, can be purchased for a small fee.

Helpline Tel. No: 0870 333 0123

20 Kings Parade, Queens Dock, Liverpool L3 4DQ
Tel: 0151 703 1500
Fax: 0151 703 1555

St Albans House, 57-60 Haymarket, London SW1Y 40X
Tel: 020 7210 4665
Fax: 020 7210 4545

Woodfield House, Tangier, Taunton, Somerset TAI 4BL
Tel: 01823 345 000
Fax: 01823 345 003

Extracts from the Register are available on the Internet, **www.charitycommission.gov.uk** however information on charitable trusts can be misleading. For example, the area of operation is based on the charity's governing document however, in practice, a charity may only operate in a small part of that area. Another example is the charity's objects, which describe what the charity has been legally set up to achieve rather than the activities carried out in order to achieve these objects. Financial information, such as annual return history and expenditure has recently been added to the site.

Publications
There are a number of national directories with information on charitable trusts (some are also available on CD-ROM). Councils for Voluntary Service, Rural Community Councils and reference libraries should have the most up-to-date copies of the printed directories.

The Directory of Grant Making Trusts
This is the most comprehensive listing of grant-making trusts nationwide and is published every two years by the Charities Aid Foundation. The 17th edition, covering 2001-2002, has information on 2,500 trusts and costs £75.00 plus £2.50 P+P from Directory of Social Change, Tel: 020 7209 5151 / Fax: 020 7209 5049 / Email: info@dsc.org.uk

A Guide to the Major Trusts (3 Volumes)
These volumes are published every two years by the Directory of Social Change. Volume 1 (8th edition, covering 2001 - 2002) has detailed information on the top 300 UK trusts, and Volume 2 (5th edition, covering 2001 – 2002) has detailed information on a further 700 trusts.
Volume 3 (2nd edition 2002) lists details on 500 UK-wide trusts.
Volumes 1 and 2 cost £19.95 plus £2 50 P+P and Volume 3 costs £17.95 + £2.50 P+P, from Directory of Social Change, Tel: 020 7209 5151 / Fax: 020 7209 5049 / Email: info@dsc.org.uk

The Directory of Grant Making Trusts and the Guide to Major Trusts series are also available on CD-ROM (annual cost: £129.24) and as a subscription based database on the web (annual cost: £129.25). Contact the Directory of Social Change for details.

Directory of Social Change Publications
DSC produce a huge range of publications, including:
- Arts Funding Guide (£16.95)
- Environmental Funding Guide (£16.95)
      European Union Funding (£12.50)
- Guide to Local Trusts in the North of England (£17.95)
- Schools Funding Guide (£16.95)
- Sports Funding Guide (£16.95)
- Youth Funding Guide (£16.95)
- Guide to Grants for Individuals In Need (£20.95)
- Educational Grants Directory (£20.95)
- Complete Fundraising Handbook (£16.95)

All of the above are available from DSC (as above). Please add £2.50 P+P.

There are many other publications about fundraising which your CVS or RCC may have available for reference.

The Internet
An increasing number of funders are putting information on the Internet - useful starting points are,
www.fundersonline.org
www. fundraising. co.uk
www.access-funds.co.uk
www.fundsnetservices.com
www.grantsonline.org.uk

FINE sends out regular bulletins with details of funding sources by e-mail please contact the office to find out more about this service or fill in the inserted page at the front of this Guide.

Other Voluntary Organisations
Voluntary organisations and community groups, both locally and nationally, who do similar work to you may already have applied to charitable trusts and therefore will have done some research on which trusts give to your sort of organisation. Some groups are not willing to give out information on who they approached but their annual report will usually contain a list of donors.

If you are a local organisation which is linked into a national network of similar groups, then your head office may be able to offer advice. It is also important to ensure that you are not applying to the same trusts as your national or regional offices.

Applications from a head office and local branches considered at the same Trustees' meetings will suggest a poor level of communication and co-ordination which reflects badly on both applications

Local Development Agencies
Councils for Voluntary Service (CVS) and Rural Community Councils (RCCs) are registered charities which operate in a specific geographical area to support the work of voluntary and community groups in that area.

Some CVS and RCCs have dedicated funding advisers and reference libraries of funding information. Most have the computer package Funderfinder, which is a searchable database of thousands of charitable trusts.

Contact your local CVS or RCC to find out what help they can give you with raising funds:
County Durham
2D: Tel: 01388 762 220
Unit 4, Crook Business Centre, New Road, Crook, Co Durham DL15 8QE

CAVOS:Tel: 01740 655 105
Cornforth House, 66 High Street, Cornforth, Co. Durham, DL17 9HS

Chester-le-Street CVS
Tel: 0191 389 1960
Volunteer Centre, Clarence Terrace, Chester-le-Street   DH3 3DQ

Darlington CVS:
Tel: 01315 480 514
Church Row, Darlington DL1 5QD

Derwentside CVS: Tel: 01207 218855
Louisa Centre, Front St, Stanley DH9 0TE

Durham City District CVS
Tel: 0191 384 4801
Office 2, IMEX Business Centre, Abbey Road, Pity Me, Durham, DH1 5JZ

Durham RCC: Tel: 01207 529621
Park House, Station Rd, Lanchester DH7 0EX

DAYCO: Tel: 0191 384 9266
The Old Schoolhouse, Front Street, Framwellgate Moor, Durham, DH1 5BL

Northumberland
Blyth Valley CVS: Tel: 01670 353623
22 Beaconsfield Street, Blyth NE24 2DP

Community Council of Northumberland: Tel: 01670 517178
Tower Buildings, 9 Oldgate, Morpeth NE61 1PY

Tynedale Voluntary Action Tel: 01434 601201
Hexham Community Centre, Gilesgate, Hexham NE46 3NP

Wansbeck CVS: Tel: 01670 858688
107 Station Road, Ashington NE63 8RS

Teesside
Hartlepool VDA: Tel: 01429 262641
Rockhaven, 36 Victoria Road, Hartlepool TS26 8DD

Middlesbrough VDA: Tel: 01642 24930
St. Mary's Centre, 82-90 Corporation Road, Middlesbrough

One Voice Tees Valley Tel: 01642 240651
New Exchange Buildings, Queens Square, Middlesbrough TS2 1AA

Redcar & Cleveland VDA Tel: 01642 440571
South Bank Health Shop, 23-27 Middlesbrough Road, South Bank, Middlesbrough TS6 6EN

Stockton Borough VDA Tel: 01642 355292
27 Yarm Road, Stockton on Tees TS18 3NJ

Tees Valley RCC: Tel: 01287 626 111
10 Dundas Street West, Saltburn, TS12 1BL

Tyne & Wear
Gateshead Voluntary Organisations Council: Tel: 0191 478 4103
John Haswell House, Gladstone Terrace, Gateshead NE8 4DY

Newcastle CVS: Tel: 0191 232 7445
MEA House, Ellison Place, Newcastle NE1 8XS

North Tyneside VODA Tel: 0191 200 5790
Linskill Centre, Linskill Terrace, North Shields NE30 2AY

South Tyneside CVS Tel: 0191 456 9551
John Hunt House, 27 Beach Road, South Shields NE33 2QA

Sunderland CVS Tel: 0191 565 1566
Riverview House, West Wear Street, Sunderland SR1 1XD

Groups outside the North East of England should contact the National Association of Councils for Voluntary Service (tel: 0114 278 6636) to find their nearest CVS or contact Action for Communities in Rural England (tel:01285 653 477) to find their nearest RCC.

Improving Your Grant Applications

Some trusts use an application form. Others specify in their guidelines what information to include and how long your application can be. The rest simply ask you to write with details of your request.

The written request is usually your only communication with the trust, so it is important to get it right before posting it.

There are two fundamental ways to improve your grant application:
• be clear
• be concise

Trusts are inundated with applications for support and those that succeed will be the ones that state the case for support in a way that is easily understood. Overstating your case will result in disappointment as the trust's correspondent will be too busy to bother to read the reams of paper you have sent them.

A good grant application involves a number of key elements:
❑ a good project
❑ a good case for support
❑ the credibility of your group / organisation
❑ the people involved in the project
❑ the interest of the funder being approached

In order to make any application clear and concise, you will need to understand your key selling points.

The most important of these are:
❑ why your work is important?
❑ who benefits from your work?
❑ how many benefit from your work?

❑ what is unique or different about your work?

Any application you make should be as brief and to the point as possible. Often only a summary of your application will be put forward to the committee that makes a decision. If your approach is by letter, it should ideally be not more than two sides of A4.

If you need to say more than this, prepare a separate covering letter on one side of A4 which summarises the project so that the funder can decide whether to consider your proposal or not.

If you are in doubt about any of the information you are sending, ask yourself the following questions:
❑ is it relevant to my application for support?
❑ will it help the funder make a decision in my favour?

In writing a letter to any potential funder you should imagine you are the person reading your application and see if you can answer the following questions:
❑ who are these people?
❑ what do they do?
❑ how much do they want and for what?
❑ why should I support them?

Other ways of improving your grant application are to ensure that it is targeted to the interests of the trust you are applying to and to send your application well before you need the money. Trusts generally make decisions through regular Trustees' meetings, which could be as infrequent as once a year, or as frequent as monthly. Some trusts will want to visit you or telephone to discuss your application in more detail before putting it to the Trustees.

Taking all of the above into consideration, not only will you improve your grant applications but also your chances of success.

The Trustees' perspective

When considering your application, Trustees will be asking themselves some or all of the following questions:

Grants Policy
1   Does the application fit within our published policy and guidelines?
2   Are we particularly interested in the problem area?
3   Is the approach to the problem the best way of spending our resources?
4   Have we funded anything similar recently?
5   Is the project within our geographical area?
6. Do we give the amount requested?

The Project
1. Will the project work?
2   Are the outcomes worthwhile and achievable?
3   Can the project staff deliver?
4. What are the long-term goals and are they achievable?
5   Is the project of purely local significance or could it have a wider benefit?
6   What is the project's relationship with clients / community / other bodies?
7   What will happen afterwards?
8   What are the long-term funding implications?

Benefit To Us If We Fund The Project
I   Is the project cost-effective? Is it better and / or cheaper than alternatives, or at least is it comparable?
2   Is the project well presented and the budget well prepared?
3   Can we guarantee the organisation will handle the money well?
4   Will the organisation say thank you and keep in regular contact (have there been any problems in the past)?
5   Will there be any publicity / recognition to us?
6. In general, will the grant be the best use of our present resources?
7   Do we know, like and trust these people?

Further Advice

Peter Ellis, our local Regional Coordinator for the **Lloyds TSB Foundation for England and Wales**, has the following advice for groups filling in the Foundation's application form:-

"Before you put pen to paper,- please use black ink – please read the Guidelines carefully to ensure your request for support falls within the work which we do. Once you have confirmed that your work does, you then need a clean sheet of paper to write down what the project is about in outline and what, if any, will be the knock on effect of carrying out that piece of work, e.g. if you are offering a training course for mothers returning to the workplace, will you need to provide a crèche facility and if so, how will that be staffed and financed. Then cost all of the project.

You then need to look at the Application Form. Read it carefully and note down what extra pieces of information you need to provide. We only want what we are asking for. We only require; a copy of your latest audited accounts and annual report, a copy of your latest bank statement, a job description if you are applying for salary support. We do not need to see anything else, e.g. constitutions. Our Question 10 asks you to list any further background information and that is what we want – a straight list of supporting information. If we need any of it we will ask you for it later.

In terms of words, we want facts and figures, which are best represented by bullet points. Look at the space for the responses. This guides you on the amount of words we want. Please be succinct. Remember – our Trustees read your Application Form. If it is handwritten, please be sure it can be easily read. If we cannot read it how can we help? If you download it from the website, remember it can be typed before you print it off.

Finally, you can telephone us for advice at any time if you are unsure about any aspect of the application process"

Further details of the policy and priorities for the Lloyds TSB Foundation for England and Wales can be found on page 110.

Peter Ellis can be contacted by writing to PO Box 779, Newcastle upon Tyne, Tyne & Wear NE99 1YJ or by telephoning 0191 261 8433 / Fax: 0191 244 6235 / Minicom: 020 7204 5442.

An example of a letter of application has been provided by John F. F Sharland, former Trust Secretary of the Sir James Knott Trust and is opposite.

AN APPLICATION FOR FUNDS

The Hamelin Rat Catching Association
29 Hatto Gardens
Lower Saxony
Tel: 020 7123 4567

Mr A Cannybody
The Secretary
Money Bags Trust
Lower Saxony

1 October 2002

Dear Mr Cannybody

REDUCTION OF BUBONIC PLAGUE – RECRUITMENT OF ADDITIONAL RAT CATCHER
APPLICATION FOR FUNDS

1. We are raising money to employ an additional rat catcher.

2. Rats are increasingly invading the Whitehall area of the town. There is no statutory rodent control organisation and no chance of statutory funding. Rat carried diseases are spreading, with an overall 10% increase in local hospital cases, in the last year 3 children are known to have died of such diseases. (Blunkett Report, May 2001).

3. Our Association is normally supported by our own fundraising events (we raised over £4,000 last year) plus appeals to local and national charities. We currently have an annual budget of only £25,000, half of which is covered by income from an invested legacy. The Lord Mayor is Chairman of our Management Committee We employ one full time rat catcher (all other workers are volunteers).

4. In order to significantly reduce the rat population, thereby reducing diseases and unnecessary child deaths, we need to recruit, train and employ a second rat catcher. The Local Health Authority have calculated that doubling the rat catching will more than halve the related diseases in the second year of operation, with further improvements in subsequent years and related benefits to the local community of a reduction in child deaths and the release of hospital beds.

5 Additional costs:	Recruiting and training	£ 3,200
	Equipment (van, pipes and telephone)	£15,000
	Annual Running costs (salary, NI, overheads)	£22 500
	First year total	**£40,700**
	Subsequent years	**£22,500 p.a. *plus inflation***

6 Our March 2002 application to the Community Fund was rejected. We intend to reapply at the earliest opportunity, but this is unlikely to be until 2003. We have already raised £2,800 locally and the Robert Browning Trust have awarded us £5,000 plus £3,000 p.a. for the next 4 years. We are asking all local trusts for help in raising the balance (preferably to cover the next 4 years) and hope to recruit in November this year. The Hatto Trust has refused, but the Hamelin Foundation are considering a grant of £1,000 p.a. for 4 years

7. I enclose last year's accounts and would be pleased to give you any more information you need. Our telephone is only manned between 3 and 5pm each weekday. Although we are not a registered charity, the Pied Charity (No. 123456) is willing to administer funds on our behalf.

8 We are particularly hopeful that you can support this appeal, as your generous donation to us in 2000 and practical support for the children's marathon put our operation on a sound footing then and the benefits this new initiative will bring to the local community relate closely to the aims of the Money Bags Trust.

P. Piper
Association Secretary

Enc Accounts FY 2001

Community Fund: North East Office by Helen Attewell, Regional Development Manager

The Community Fund, formerly known as the National Lottery Charities Board, began giving grants in 1995 and has awarded £119 million to over 2,000 voluntary organisations in the North East in the first seven years. The money is raised through 4.7p of every £1 spent on the National Lottery and the North East receives more per head than any other English region because of the relative levels of deprivation here.

Our overall mission is to support projects that help meet the needs of the most disadvantaged people. We are particularly interested in projects that help tackle severe, long term and multiple needs. We will also make grants which improve the quality of life in the community.

The Community Fund was set up by parliament, which affects what we can do and the way we work. For example, we can only make grants to organisations which are established for charitable, benevolent or philanthropic purposes. You do not have to be a registered charity to apply, but you must have a constitution or set of rules which we will look at to make sure you are eligible. More information on this is available from the website or the regional office and we can check whether you are eligible before you make a full application.

The Community Fund remains a generalist grant-giver, although with the launch of our 5 year Strategic Plan

in April 2002, we are increasingly looking to target our resources at our local priorities under six corporate beneficiary groups; **Older people and their carers, Disabled people and their carers, Black and minority ethnic communities, Children and young people, Refugees and asylum seekers and the 20% most deprived wards in the region.** We also prioritise applications from groups working in our Fair Share areas (Darlington and Stockton), as well as infrastructure and capacity building projects which are focused on our priority groups. Please see our website to download a copy of "Our aims and priorities".

We have two grant programmes; Grants for large projects (up to £300,000) and Grants for medium sized projects (up to £60,000 – NB this applies to the project as a whole, not just the Community Fund contribution). In addition the Community Fund contributes to the lottery funding joint pot for small grants of £500 to £5,000, administered by Awards for All. We encourage new applicants to obtain a copy of "Before you Apply" as a helpful tool to establish whether you are eligible for Community Fund grants and to plan your project. Once you have worked through the checklist on the back which details the type of evidence you will have to gather to support your application, you are encouraged to fill out the appropriate form. Our application packs contain detailed information about our policies and come with extensive help notes to assist you in completing the form. We publish three sets of guidance for property applications and a series of checklists appropriate to different types of property bids. You can also make an appointment to come along to a surgery session and discuss your application with a Community Fund member of staff.

The regional office has a team of staff who assess applications, monitor grants made and undertake development work. Applications are assessed by Grants Officers, with final recommendations by a local Regional Committee, made up of people from the region with a range of local experience and knowledge. Consultation and partnership links continue with many voluntary organisations and statutory bodies in the North East, which will continue to inform our work and priorities over the lifetime of the Strategic Plan and beyond.

For advice and information contact:
Community Fund
North East Regional Office
6th Floor
Baron House
4 Neville Street
Newcastle upon Tyne
NE1 5NL

Tel: 0191 255 1133
Fax: 0191 233 1997
Minicom: 0191 233 2099
Email:
enquiries@ne.community-fund.org.uk
Website: www.community-fund.org.uk

For "Before you Apply, an application pack or guidance notes contact:

Tel: 0845 791 9191
Textphone: 0845 655 6656
Website: www.community-fund.org.uk

The Northern Rock Foundation
By Fiona Ellis, Director

New home, new image and new guidelines for the Northern Rock Foundation.

In 2003 we will look different and we will be in a new building. We are also changing our grants programmes. Why? Well our building is too small – we have not even got our own Board room never mind rooms in which to meet applicants – and it is not very accessible so we have to move. Our logo and our visual materials need a bit of refreshing; they were done in a hurry that's why the logo says The Northern Rock Foundation twice!

As for the grants programmes, there are several good reasons for changing them. Before I say what they are let me do a quick bit of reassurance. Not quite everything is being abandoned. Over the past five years we have learned a lot. Some organisations which have already received grants will see from the new application pack that they still fit into the new programmes. Others alas will not. "Every choice is a sacrifice." That means if we are to stick to our aim of reaching previously excluded applicants we have to give up some of those we have already helped.

We need to change because we made that commitment early on – to try, over time, to reach as many voluntary sector areas as possible. Readers in the North East will also be pleased to learn that we are to change our area of benefit – it was getting messy so now we will only fund in the North East and Cumbria. These areas are to be on a totally equal base for all main grant programmes. We have been wondering too about what our grants accomplish and in order to help applicants and ourselves, to think about this more clearly from the very beginning, we have described our programmes according to the effects we want people to achieve.

As always it will take a little time for these programmes to bed down. We hope not to have to change the guidelines again for at least a few years, but our ability to fund all comers will sharpen our decisions in time.

Details of grants available from The Northern Rock Foundation can be found on p.121 of this guide.

County Durham Foundation by Gillian Stacey, Director

What is the County Durham Foundation?

County Durham Foundation is an independent grant making charity. Our purpose is to support community based projects that make a real difference to the quality of life for local people and particularly those who are disadvantaged. Since our launch in 1995, we have grown rapidly and last year we distributed nearly £1 million in grants, primarily in County Durham and Darlington.

We act as a vehicle for individuals, families and companies who want to put something back into their local community. We offer advice on the best way to make a donation work for the beneficiaries and the most tax efficient ways to give. Uniquely, we endeavour to match the interests of our donors with the needs of the community and to offer donors a say in how their gift is used.

We also attract substantial amounts of flow through funding and now operate grant programmes on behalf of bodies such as Government Office North East (GONE) and central government departments such as the Active Community Unit and Children's and Young People's Unit. We also operate a Millennium Awards scheme on behalf of the Millennium Commission with money from the National Lottery.

This means that we have some restrictions on our grant making and therefore cannot fund every project or group that we would like to. To make it easier for potential applicants to determine whether they should apply or not, we have issued a new Group Applications booklet which details every fund available. Please read our entry in this guide (page 66) and our full information for Group Applicants booklet, which you can get by calling the office, (Tel: 0191 383 0055), or by logging on to our website at; www.countydurhamfoundation.co.uk

We would really appreciate if you would follow this advice so as to prevent any waste of our and your time and money.

We focus on small grant making, with an average grant size being £1,300. This is a small grant programme for small local groups. Every programme we manage has its own criteria, but all use the same application form. If you don't know which fund you wish to apply for, we will work it out behind the scenes. Unless your application is ineligible, you will receive a telephone call from one of our grant assessors to ask you further questions or to clarify information. Please ensure that the contact person on the application form is the one most knowledgeable of and able to talk about your project. If your application is complete, you will hear within three months whether you are successful.

Decisions on the success of your grant will be taken by a variety of grants committees, many of which are district based and involve former grant recipients and applicants.

Most groups that are unsuccessful in gaining a grant from County Durham Foundation fail for the following reasons:
• they did not fit the criteria;

• the application was incomplete, e.g. there was no constitution, accounts or a proper budget;
• that additional information requested or omitted information requested by County Durham Foundation staff was not sent;
• the application did not have the support of the local community or the local group;
• there was no tangible community benefit;
• the group had not demonstrated that they had sufficient capacity to manage the grant, (this is most likely an issue with very small groups which have not previously applied for a grant of significant size);
• the application was for a small contribution towards a large project.

If your application is incomplete, it could mean that as a group you are not ready for a grant and your trustees may need to develop further skills or the group further procedures. You can contact your local Council for Voluntary Service for help and advice before submitting your application.

Last but not least, we are not looking for perfectly written applications. There are no magic buzzwords which will automatically ensure your success. Some of our best grants were given because the enthusiasm and commitment of the applicant shone through in their telephone assessment, despite a poorly written application.

We are interested in supporting good groups and projects that have the potential and enthusiasm to improve. So if you fit the bill, we look forward to receiving your application!

Meeting Dates of Trusts

Make sure your application arrives six to eight weeks before the Trustees next meet.

January
- Abbey National Charitable Trust
- John Bell Charitable Trust
- The Hospital of God at Greatham
- Hadrian Trust
- The Joicey Trust
- R W Mann Trustees Limited
- Sir John Priestman Charity Trust
- The Royal Victoria Trust for the Blind
- The St Hilda's Trust
- The TFM Cash Challenge Appeal
- The Tubney Charitable Trust
- Washington Community Development Trust
- Garfield Weston Charitable Trust
- The Women's Trust Fund

February
- Abbey National Charitable Trust
- The Sir James Knott Trust
- The Allen Lane Foundation
- R W Mann Trustees Limited
- The Rothley Trust
- Washington Community Development Trust
- The Weavers Company Benevolent Fund
- Garfield Weston Charitable Trust

March
- Abbey National Charitable Trust
- BBC Children In Need Appeal
- The Percy Bilton Charity (grants over £500)
- The Calouste Gulbenkian Foundation (UK Branch)
- Children's Foundation
- Church Urban Fund
- Exclusive Charity Haggerston Owners (ECHO)
- The Four Winds Trust
- The Joseph Strong Frazer Trust
- The Goshen Trust
- Hadrian Trust
- The W A Handley Charity Trust
- R W Mann Trustees Limited
- The Royal Victoria Trust for the Blind
- The Sedgefield Charities
- Shaftoe Educational Foundation
- The Henry Smith Charity
- Wallsend Charitable Trust
- Washington Community Development Trust
- The William Webster Charitable Trust
- Garfield Weston Charitable Trust
- The 1989 Willan Charitable Trust
- Yapp Charitable Trusts

April
- Abbey National Charitable Trust
- The Continuation Charitable Trust
- Exclusive Charity Haggerston Owners (ECHO)
- R W Mann Trustees Limited
- Sir John Priestman Charity Trust
- The St Hilda's Trust
- The Tubney Charitable Trust
- Washington Community Development Trust
- Garfield Weston Charitable Trust

May
- Abbey National Charitable Trust
- Lord Crewe's Charity
- Exclusive Charity Haggerston Owners (ECHO)
- The Hospital of God at Greatham
- Greggs Trust (major grants)
- R W Mann Trustees Limited
- The Leslie and Lillian Manning Trust
- The Millfield House Foundation
- The Rothley Trust
- The Royal Victoria Trust for the Blind

- Washington Community Development Trust
- Garfield Weston Charitable Trust

June
- Abbey National Charitable Trust
- The Percy Bilton Charity (grants over £500)
- Church Urban Fund
- Exclusive Charity Haggerston Owners (ECHO)
- The Goshen Trust
- The W A Handley Charity Trust
- The Sir James Knott Trust
- The Allen Lane Foundation
- R W Mann Trustees Limited
- The Henry Smith Charity
- The Baily Thomas Charitable Fund
- Wallsend Charitable Trust
- Washington Community Development Trust
- The Weavers Company Benevolent Fund
- Garfield Weston Charitable Trust
- The 1989 Willan Charitable Trust

July
- Abbey National Charitable Trust
- The Calouste Gulbenkian Foundation (UK Branch)
- Exclusive Charity Haggerston Owners (ECHO)
- The Hospital of God at Greatham
- Hadrian Trust
- The Joicey Trust
- R W Mann Trustees Limited
- Sir John Priestman Charity Trust
- The Ropner Centenary Trust
- The Royal Victoria Trust for the Blind
- Rural Youth Trust
- The St Hilda's Trust
- The Storrow Scott Charitable Will Trust
- Shaftoe Educational Foundation
- The Smith (Haltwhistle & District) Trust

- The TFM Cash Challenge Appeal
- The Tubney Charitable Trust
- Washington Community Development Trust
- The William Webster Charitable Trust
- Garfield Weston Charitable Trust
- The Women's Trust Fund
- Yapp Charitable Trusts

August
- Abbey National Charitable Trust
- Exclusive Charity Haggerston Owners (ECHO)
- R W Mann Trustees Limited
- The Rothley Trust
- Washington Community Development Trust
- Garfield Weston Charitable Trust

September
- Abbey National Charitable Trust
- The Percy Bilton Charity (grants over £500)
- Church Urban Fund
- Exclusive Charity Haggerston Owners (ECHO)
- The Joseph Strong Frazer Trust
- The Goshen Trust
- The W A Handley Charity Trust
- R W Mann Trustees Limited
- Christopher Rowbotham Charitable Trust
- The Royal Victoria Trust for the Blind
- The Henry Smith Charity
- Wallsend Charitable Trust
- Washington Community Development Trust
- Garfield Weston Charitable Trust
- The 1989 Willan Charitable Trust

October
- Abbey National Charitable Trust
- The Continuation Charitable Trust
- Exclusive Charity Haggerston Owners (ECHO)

- The Hospital of God at Greatham
- Hadrian Trust
- The Sir James Knott Trust
- The Allen Lane Foundation
- R W Mann Trustees Limited
- The St Hilda's Trust
- The Sedgefield Charities
- The Tubney Charitable Trust
- Washington Community Development Trust
- The Weavers Company Benevolent Fund
- Garfield Weston Charitable Trust

November
- Abbey National Charitable Trust
- BBC Children In Need Appeal
- The Calouste Gulbenkian Foundation (UK Branch)
- Children's Foundation
- Lord Crewe's Charity
- Gregg's Trust (major grants)
- R W Mann Trustees Limited
- The Leslie and Lillian Manning Trust
- The Millfield House Foundation
- Northumberland Village Homes Trust
- The Rothley Trust
- The Royal Victoria Trust for the Blind
- Shaftoe Educational Foundation
- The Tyneside Charitable Trust
- Washington Community Development Trust
- The William Webster Charitable Trust
- Garfield Weston Charitable Trust
- The 1989 Willan Charitable Trust
- Yapp Charitable Trusts

December
- Abbey National Charitable Trust
- The Percy Bilton Charity (grants over £500)
- Church Urban Fund
- The Goshen Trust
- The W A Handley Charity Trust

- R W Mann Trustees Limited
- The Ropner Centenary Trust
- Rural Youth Trust
- The Henry Smith Charity
- The Baily Thomas Charitable Fund
- Wallsend Charitable Trust
- Washington Community Development Trust
- Garfield Weston Charitable Trust

No Meeting Dates Specified
- The Ayton Charitable Trust (quarterly)
- The Barbour Trust (Grants up to £500 – monthly, Grants over £500 – quarterly)
- The Baring Foundation (differs for different programmes)
- The Benfield Motors Charitable Trust (twice a year)
- The Percy Bilton Charity (grants of up to £500 are considered on an ongoing basis, Grants over £500 - quarterly)
- The J H Burn Charity
- CDENT Environment and Waste Fund
- The Camelot Foundation (four times a year)
- Century Radio Limited Charitable Trust
- Charities Aid Foundation (differs for different programmes)
- The Chase Charity (quarterly)
- The De Clermont Charitable Company Limited (continuously)
- Cleveland Community Foundation (differs for different programmes)
- Coalfields Regeneration Trust (every six weeks)
- Comic Relief (8 times a year)
- Community Foundation serving Tyne & Wear and Northumberland (meetings throughout the year)
- Catherine Cookson Trust
- County Durham Foundation (differs for different programmes)

- Cumberland Building Society Charitable Foundation (quarterly)
- Diana, Princess of Wales Memorial Fund (twice a year)
- Hedley Denton Charitable Trust (twice a year)
- Dickon Trust
- Esmee Fairbairn Foundation
- Foundation for Sport and the Arts (2 sets of meetings per year)
- Maurice Fry Charitable Trust
- J Paul Getty Jr General Charitable Trust (quarterly)
- The Hanson Environment Fund (quarterly for the main fund & monthly for community scheme grants)
- John Haswell Memorial Fund (every two months)
- Bill & May Hodgson Charitable Trust (once a year)
- The Ruth & Lionel Jacobson Charitable Trust (every two months)
- The Rose Joicey Fund
- The Kelly Charitable Trust (infrequently, as required)
- The Lankelly Foundation (quarterly)
- The William Leech Charity (6 times a year)
- Lloyds TSB Foundation for England and Wales (quarterly)
- The Mahila Fund (once a year)
- The Sir Stephen Middleton Charity Trust (quarterly)
- Northern Electric Employees Charity Association (every ten weeks)
- The Northern Rock Foundation (at least five times a year)
- Northumberland Foundation for Young People (quarterly)
- Northumberland Rugby Union Charitable Trust
- Northumbria Historic Churches Trust (quarterly)
- The Ragdoll Foundation (four times a year)
- The Rank Foundation (quarterly)
- The Ravenscroft Foundation (as often as necessary)
- The Ropner Trust (quarterly)
- Shears Charitable Trust
- The Sherburn House Charity (every two months)
- SITA Environmental Trust (every eight weeks)
- The Bernard Sunley Charitable Foundation (quarterly)
- Teesside Emergency Relief Fund (usually monthly)
- Thompson's of Prudhoe Environmental Trust (quarterly)
- The Tudor Trust (continuously throughout the year)
- The Vardy Foundation
- York Diocese Social Care Fund (quarterly)
- Yorkshire Agricultural Society (quarterly)
- Yorkshire Bank Charitable Trust (every six to eight weeks)

The Abbey National Charitable Trust

Correspondent	Alan Eagle
	Trust Secretary
	PO Box 911
	Milton Keynes
	MK9 1AD
Telephone	0870 608 0104
Fax	01908 348339

E-mail
communitypartnership@
abbeynational.co.uk

Website
www.abbeynational.com

CC No	2509711
Income	£1,967,804 (2001)
Grants	£2,075,744 (2001)
Trustees	The Trust has 10 Trustees at any one time
Area	UK
Meets	Monthly

Policy
The Trust makes one-off grants of between £50 and £20,000 to registered charities. The Trustees are committed to empowering disadvantaged people to live fuller lives.

Absolute priority is given to the following inter-related areas:

Equal Opportunities for Disabled People
This area covers special equipment, access, housing, participation in sport and the arts. The Trust aims to help people with physical disabilities, sensory impairments, as well as learning disabilities, mental illness and infirmity owing to old age.

Education for Disadvantaged Groups
The priority in this area is to help people of any age with special educational or training needs. This includes minority ethnic communities, disabled people, homeless people or inner city social exclusion projects. Private schools other than for special needs are not supported.

Employment for Disadvantaged Groups
The same priority groups apply, minority ethnic communities, disabled people, homeless people or inner city social exclusion projects. Youth unemployment may be added to this.

The Trust favour smaller charities or local appeals from national charities.

Grants
The Trust made grants totalling £2,075,744 during 2001, the following were made to North East organisations:
- Scope on Teesside - £3,500
- Cleveland Domestic Violence Forum - £2,100
- Darlington Association on Disability - £1,950
- Stockton Speech After Stroke – £1,500
- Olan Pons Community Association - £5,000
- Gatham House - £4,900
- Stockton Borough Carers Resource
- Centre – £1,792

Applications
Applications are in writing to the correspondent. Guidelines are available from the Trust and telephone calls to discuss applications are welcome.

The Abbey National Charitable Trust (Cont..)

Applicants should include details of what the donation is required for and an explanation of how this meets the Trust's priorities.

Applications for over £1,000 must include a business plan and a copy of the latest accounts. It is also helpful to include supporting information such as a recent newsletter or annual report. Applications are not acknowledged, however all applicants will be informed of the outcome of their application. Successful applicants will be required to provide the Trust with an annual report for monitoring and evaluation purposes.

Successful applicants are required to wait for 2 years before re-applying. Unsuccessful applicants may re-apply after 1 year.

Exclusions
The Trust **does not** make donations which:
- Benefit or sponsor specific individuals
- Support lobbying or political parties
- Would benefit principally a single religious or ethnic group
- Are to help causes outside the UK
- Are to replace statutory funding
- Last for more than 1 year
- Are to support fundraising by individuals or other grant making bodies
- Are circular appeals

Ayton Charitable Trust

Correspondent	J T M Ayton Trustee Potters Well 13 Quarry Heads Lane Durham DH1 3DY
Telephone	0191 386 4803
CC No	326687
Income	£18,075 (2001/02)
Grants	£17,902 (2001/02)
Trustees	V Ayton, A M Ayton, A J Hyde, J T M Ayton
Area	Mainly County Durham
Meets	Quarterly

Policy
The Trust does not have a written policy but considers each application carefully.

Grants
The Trust awarded 27 grants, totalling £17,902 in the year ending 5th April 2002. Grants ranged from £52 to £2,000.
The following are examples:
- Botton Village - £500
- Durham Samaritans - £500
- Durham High School - £1,000
- North East Prison After Care
- Service - £650
- Waddington Street United
- Reform Church - £2,000

Ayton Charitable Trust (Cont..)

Applications
Applications should be made in writing to the correspondent.

Exclusions
No grants are made to individuals.

Helpful Hint...

Make every word work for you – you have limited space to get your message across and the attention span of the reader will be short.

The Barbour Charitable Trust

Correspondent	Mrs A Harvey PO Box 21 Guisborough Cleveland TS14 8YH
Telephone	0191 455 4444
CC No	328081
Income	Variable
Grants	Variable
Trustees	Dame Margaret Barbour DBE DL, Mr A A E Glenton, Mr H J Tavroges, Miss Helen Barbour,
Secretary	Mrs E Howse
Administrator	Mrs A Harvey
Area	Tyne and Wear and Northumberland
Meets	Small grants up to £500 – monthly Large grants over £500 – quarterly

Policy
Grants normally range from £500 to up to £50,000. The majority of grants are under £500.

The Trust makes grants to: Registered charitable organisations whose objectives include:
- The promotion of research into the cause and treatment of illness or disease and the provision of medical equipment.

The Barbour Charitable Trust (Cont..)

- The protection and preservation for the benefit of the public in the North East of England such features of cities, towns, villages and the countryside as are of special environmental, historical and architectural interest.
- The relief of persons resident in the North East of England who are in condition of need, hardship or distress as a result of local, national or international disaster, or by reasons of their social and economic circumstances.
- To help improve the employment prospects of young people and to alleviate their problems of homelessness in the North East of England.

The Trust always receives more applications than it has funds to support. Even if a project fits the Trust's policy priorities, it may not be possible to make a grant.

Grants
In the year 1999 / 2000 more than 700 grants were made, these included:
- North Tyneside Motor Project –
- £250
- Northumbria Coalition Against Crime - £500
- Bliss=ability (South Shields) –
- £2,000

Applications
Applications are in writing to the correspondent. The applications should include full back-up information, a statement of accounts and the official charity number of the applicant.

Exclusions
The Trust **cannot** consider:
- Requests from outside the area
- Requests from educational establishments
- Individual applications unless backed by a particular charitable organisation
- Capital grants for building projects.

The Baring Foundation

Correspondent	Toby Johns
	Director
	60 London Wall
	London
	EC2M 5TQ
Telephone	020 7767 1348
Fax	020 7767 7121
E-mail	baring.foundation@uk.ing.com
Website	www.baringfoundation.org.uk
CC No	258583
Income	£2,150,473 (2001)
Grants	£3,564,770 (2001)
Trustees	N H Baring, T Baring CBE, R D Broadley, M Findlay, A Lewis-Jones, A D Loehins CMG, J R Peers, Sir C Tickell CGMG KCVO
Area	England and Wales
Meets	Each Grants Programme has its own schedule of meetings to assess applications; further details are given in the Guidelines.

Policy

The starting point for all the Foundation's grant-making activity is a belief in the importance to the whole community of having an active, well informed and ably led voluntary sector, nationally and locally. The Foundation concentrates its efforts on helping strengthen organisations' capacity and confidence to respond effectively to changes in funding or government policy, to identify and tackle new opportunities or challenges and to manage their affairs in ways that ensure their charitable purposes are efficiently and competently fulfilled.

Around 60% of the Foundation's grants budget until the end of 2001 was committed to supporting the central core running of selected voluntary organisations, particularly those which have limited opportunities to raise money from the general public and "infrastructure" organisations, to be kept well informed about developments and issues across the charitable sector. These core grants are only given to organisations chosen by the Foundation's Council members – please do not apply for a core grant.

Strengthening the Voluntary Sector Grants Programme
Only supports national organisations and local organisations in Devon, Cornwall, London and Merseyside.

Arts Programme
This aims to recognise and encourage good practice in the provision of opportunities to participate in the Arts. Again, there is a Core Costs Fund (open only to those invited by the Foundation to apply). There are also Project Grants of up to £7,000 for constituted, not-for-profit organisations working in education or community settings. This programme is open to applications from national and local arts organisations anywhere in England and Wales.

International Grants Programme
Details for this programme will be available on the Foundation website from Autumn 2002.

The Baring Foundation (Cont..)

Grants

The Foundation made 145 grants in 2001, totalling £3.56million. A full list of these grants is available on the website.

One major grant was made in the North East of England in 2001, £75,000 was awarded to Cleveland Arts.

Applications

Guidelines and application forms for each Grants Programme and Fund are available from the Foundation's office and website. Please read the Guidelines carefully to see if you are excluded from applying and, if not, when you need to submit your application by, what is likely to happen once you have submitted your application and how long it could take before you hear whether you have been successful or not. The Guidelines will also tell you when you can re-apply to the same Fund.

Exclusions

Each Grants Programme has its own Exclusions – please check Guidelines carefully.

BBC Children In Need

Correspondent	Mrs M Milburn PO Box 76 London W3 6FS
CC No	802052
Telephone	0208 576 7788
Fax	0208 576 8887
Email	pudsey@bbc.co.uk
Website	www.bbc.co.uk/pudsey
Income	£22,054,477
Grants	£20,670,408
Trustees	T Cook, W Day, A Duncan, L Heggessey, R Jones OBE, D L Jordan, M Kershaw, N Mahal, S Milner, L Rylatt, A Sarkis, P Wicks, T Wogan OBE
Area	UK
Meets	Twice a year (applications must be received by 30 November or 30 March each year)

Policy

BBC Children In Need raises money to help children aged 18 years and under in the UK who fall into one or more of the following categories:
- Any kind of disability
- Behavioural or psychological problems

BBC Children In Need (Cont..)

- Living in poverty or situations of deprivation illness, distress, abuse or neglect

Properly constituted, not for profit groups (e.g. self help groups, voluntary organisations, registered charities) can apply for salary and revenue grants for up to three years (N.B. rarely for amounts over £25,000 a year) or for one-off grants for capital projects, seasonal projects (e.g. holiday playschemes), holidays / outings, equipment and welfare funds. Grants for individual children are only made through organisations which apply on their behalf and which can vouch for the financial and other circumstances of the family.
Projects should have a clear focus on changing the lives of disadvantaged children for the better.

Grants
During 2000/2001, BBC Children In Need awarded 1,830 grants, totalling £20,670,408.

There were 158 grants made in the North East, totalling £1,781,706, including:
- Home Start Kirklees - £1,400
- West Walker Community Association - £1,174
- St Agnes Playgroup - £1,048
- 9th Billingham Scouts Group - £1,045
- Priory Lane Out Of School Club - £1,000
- Learning Library Durham - £1,000
- CVS Blyth Valley - £1,000
- Hexham Youth Initiative - £14,017
- Hartlepool Families First - £19,905
- Women's Aid Wear Valley - £30,000
- Pennywell Neighbourhood Centre - £29,302

Applications
Guidelines and application forms are updated every year - please check you have the most up to date versions. You need to be clear about what the problem is and how your project will do something about it, giving relevant facts and figures. Show what you can realistically achieve. Please avoid using jargon. Your budget should show that you've done your homework and know what things cost.

If you are applying for staff salaries, it is important to show your experience as an employer or your plans to acquire the management skills you need and to enclose a job description, person specification and work plan for the first year of the grant. All new posts funded by BBC Children In Need should be publicly advertised, unless for short term or seasonal staff.

In 2002/2003, there are two closing dates for applications - 30 November 2002 and 30 March 2003.

Organisations may submit only one application and can apply to only one of these two dates. Applications for summer projects must be received by the November of the previous year.

Applicants should allow up to five months from each closing date for a written decision.

Organisations may hold only one grant at a time from BBC Children In Need and no further applications can be considered until you submit a report on the use of the previous grant.

Exclusions
Grants are **not** given for:
- Trips abroad or projects abroad
- Medical treatment or medical research
- Unspecified expenditure

BBC Children In Need (Cont..)

- Deficit funding or the repayment of loans
- Projects which take place before applications can be processed
- Projects which are unable to start within 12 months distribution to another / other organisation(s)
- General appeals and endowment funds
- The relief of statutory responsibilities

Helpful Hint...

Ask for a specific amount of money – it will give funders a better idea of how to gauge the size of grant to give.

John Bell Charitable Trust

Correspondent	R I Stewart Trustee 2 Broadway Tynemouth NE30 2LD
CC No	272631
Income	£23,154 (2001/02)
Grants	£30,250 (2001/02)
Trustees	R I Stewart, N Sherlock, H Straker
Area	Northumberland, County Durham and Tyne and Wear
Meets	Once a year (in January / February)

Policy
The Trust makes one-off grants towards core and project revenue costs of organisations operating in the North East of England. Social welfare organisations working with children / young people and the elderly are often supported, as are schools, hospices / hospitals and environmental groups.

Grants
Grants totalling £30,250 were awarded in the year ending 5th April 2002. These included:
- Gujarati Earthquake Appeal - £1,000
- Durham County Scout Association - £2,000
- Cedarwood Trust - £1,000
- A.D.A.P.T - £1,000
- Northumberland County Scout Association - £2,000
- Hadrian District Scout Council- £1,000

John Bell Charitable Trust (Cont..)

- Percy Hedley Foundation - £1,000
- The Calvert Trust - £1,000
- The Community Foundation - £1,000
- Cancer Bridge - £2,000
- Common Wealth Youth Appeal - £2,000
- Fairbridge in Tyne & Wear - £1,000
- Great North Air Ambulance Appeal - £2,000
- St. Chads Community Programme £2,000
- Wesley Memorial Methodist Church - £1,000
- Kirkwhelpington P.C.C. - £1,000
- Royal Agricultural Benevolent Society - £2,000
- Christ Church with St. Ann - £1,000

Applications
Apply in writing to the correspondent. Applications are not acknowledged and only successful applicants are informed of the outcome of their application.

Exclusions
None supplied.

Benfield Motors Charitable Trust

Correspondent	Mrs L Squires Trustee Asama Court Newcastle Business Park Newcastle upon Tyne NE4 7YD
Telephone	0191 226 1700
CC No	328149
Income	No information available
Grants	£39,393 (1996/97)
Trustees	J Squires, M Squires, S Squires, L Squires
Area	Preference for the North East of England
Meets	Twice a year

Policy
The Trust did not respond to requests, for information therefore the entry is based on information previously held by FINE.

Grants are mainly given to health and welfare and Christian charities.

Grants
In the year ending 16 March 1997, The Trust awarded 60 grants, totalling £39,393. Grants ranged from £10 to £10,000 and included:
- Tyne & Wear Foundation - £10,000
- St Oswald's Hospice - £6,633
- Northumbria Coalition Against Crime - £2,000
- Benfield School - £894
- Fairbridge in Tyne & Wear - £500

Benfield Motors Charitable Trust (Cont..)

- NE Pensioners Association - £100
- Gosforth Friday Club - £25

FINE has a full list of all grants made.

Applications
In writing to the correspondent.

Exclusions
No details supplied.

Percy Bilton Charity

Correspondent	Miss P Ponnaiyah Company Secretary Bilton House 58 Uxbridge Road Ealing London W5 2TL
Telephone	020 8579 2829
Fax	020 8567 5459
CC No	212474
Income	£697,304 (2002)
Grants	£775,935 (2002)
Trustees	W J D Moberly, M A Bilton, W J Uzielli, J R Lee
Area	UK
Meets	Quarterly, in March, June, September, December. Applications for small grants of up to £500 are considered on an ongoing basis.

Policy
Grants are available only for capital expenditure. Only registered charities or youth organisations may apply for funding. The Trust is interested in supporting the following kinds of projects:

Disadvantaged / Underprivileged Young People (Persons Under 25)
- To assist with and alleviate problems facing young people who are educationally and socially underprivileged, disadvantaged or marginalised.

Percy Bilton Charity (Cont..)

- To encourage young people into education, training, supported living and employment away from crime, substance misuse and alcohol dependence, homelessness and unemployment.
- To provide facilities for recreational activities and outdoor pursuits for young people who are educationally and socially underprivileged or disadvantaged.

People with Disabilities (physical, mental or learning)

- To provide suitable facilities for residential / respite care, occupational and recreational establishments for children, young people and adults with physical or learning disabilities or enduring mental health problems.
- To encourage those with the above disabilities to gain a greater degree of independence.

Older People (aged over 60)

- To provide day centres, nursing and residential homes, sheltered accommodation and respite care for the frail and sufferers of dementia or age related disorders.
- To alleviate poverty and hardship, relief of isolation and loneliness among older people.
- To assist older people to maintain independent or supported living.

There are two main types of funding available:

Main Funding – single grants for capital expenditure in excess of £2,000. In the case of major building / refurbishment appeals applications should be made after 75% of the funding has been secured.

Small Grants – donations of up to £500 towards furnishings and equipment for small projects.

Grants
Grants made include:
- Trinity Youth Association - £1,870
- Northern Counties School for the Deaf - £5,000
- Gateway Wheelers, County Durham - £450
- Leadgate Community Tearooms Association, County Durham - £470
- Springwell Monday Club, Gateshead - £328
- 2510 (West Denton) Squadron Air Training Corps - £200
- Cullercoats Skater Hockey Club, North Tyneside - £300
- South Tyneside Women's Aid - £200

Applications
Applications can be made at any time, but the Trustees only make decisions on grants quarterly, except for grants under £500 which are considered on an ongoing basis.

For main funding written applications, on letter headed paper, should include:
- A brief history and outline of your charity
- Description of the project and its principal aims
- Details of funding, including: for equipment appeals – a list of items required with costs
- A budget for the project including details of funds already raised and other sources being approached
- Statement of cost or costs involved for a building / refurbishment project – please itemise major items and professional fees if applicable
- Building or other plans. Please state whether all relevant planning

Percy Bilton Charity (Cont..)

consents and building regulations approvals have been obtained
- Timetable of construction / refurbishment and anticipated date of completion
- State whether the project has ongoing revenue funding
- Proposals for monitoring and evaluating the project
- A copy of the most recent annual report and audited accounts

When applying for a small grant, applications should also be in writing on letter headed paper and include:
- Brief details of the aims of your organisation
- Outline of the project and its principal aims
- Costs of the items required
- If your organisation is not a registered charity please obtain a reference from a youth organisation, a charity that you work with or a Council for Voluntary Service
- A copy of the latest audited accounts

Applications for small grants should be addressed to the Small Grants Committee and those for main funding to The Administrator.

Successful and unsuccessful applicants can reapply after 18 months.

Exclusions
The Charity **does not** consider:
- Running expenses for the organisations or individual projects
- Salaries or office furniture / equipment
- Donations for general funding
- Play schemes / summer schemes
- Holidays or expeditions for individuals or groups
- Trips, activities or events

- Community centres or village halls for wider community use
- Community sports / play area facilities
- Pre-schools or play groups (other than for disabled children)
- Refurbishment or repair of places of worship / church halls
- Research projects
- The Arts (Theatre, Dance Groups, etc.)
- Schools, Colleges or Universities (other than special schools)
- Welfare funds or other grant making bodies for distribution
- Hospital / medical equipment
- Disabled access to facilities used predominantly by the able bodied
- Works to premises used primarily by those not within the criteria
- Projects that have been completed
- Items already purchased.

J H Burn Charity Trust

Correspondent	D R B Burn Carrycoats Hall Wark Hexham Northumberland NE48 3JG
CC No	226320
Income	£5,275 (2001)
Grants	£5,075 (2001)
Trustees	D R B Burn, S D Burn
Area	Northumberland, Newcastle upon Tyne and Durham
Meets	No information supplied

Policy
The Trust makes one-off grants to registered charities and specifies its areas of giving as:
- General charitable purposes
- Sailors and seamen (including lifeboats)
- Religion (the provision and upkeep of places of worship)
- Hospitals and nursing
- Art galleries
- Boys clubs

Grants
No information supplied.

Applications
Applications should be made in writing. They will not be acknowledged and there is no need to enclose a stamped addressed envelope with your application. Applicants should quote their registered charity number.

Exclusions
No grants are made to individuals.

Helpful Hint...

Do your research !! The more you know about the trust and how your project or proposal meets its criteria, the more likely you are to succeed.

Calouste Gulbenkian Foundation (UK Branch)

Correspondent	Paula Ridley Director 98 Portland Place London W1B 1ET
Telephone	020 7636 5313
Fax	020 7908 7580
E-mail	info@gulbenkian.org.uk
Website	www.gulbenkian.org.uk
Grants	£2,327,888 (2001)
Trustees	The Foundation's Board of Administration in Lisbon
Area	UK and Republic of Ireland
Meets	Three times a year (usually March, July and November)

Policy

The Foundation outlines it's priorities for grant making in the leaflet "Advice to Applicants for Grants for UK and Ireland", available from the Foundation Office.

The work of the Foundation is divided into programmes – Arts, Education, Social Welfare and Anglo-Portuguese cultural Relations. The Foundation has a history of supporting pioneering developments. Applications from outside London are especially welcome.

The following guidelines are taken from the Foundation's leaflet dated January 2002; please check that this is the most up to date leaflet before applying.

Arts (Assistant Director, Sian Ede)
The Arts Programme deals with arts for adults and young people out of formal education settings. It has three priority areas.

- The Spoken Word – this programme is designed to heighten an awareness of the richness and variety of spoken language in Contemporary Britain. Applications are invited for innovative projects which principally involve non-professional practitioners, especially groups which demonstrate social need. Projects may involve any of the following media: oral history collection, community radio, poetry to be spoken aloud or the development of dialogue in drama, fiction and documentary.
- The Arts and Science – designed to encourage professional arts organisations to establish projects which engage with new thinking and practice in science and technology.
- Tryout and Experiment – offers a small number of grants to groups of practitioners to try out ideas in the studio or rehearsal room in advance of normal rehearsal or preparation time.

Potential applications should be submitted at least three months before the starting date of the project.

Calouste Gulbenkian Foundation (Cont..)

Education (Assistant Director, Simon Richey)
There are 2 strands within this programme:

Educational Innovations and Developments covers:

- Helping Schools, Helping Parents - aims to help primary and secondary schools assist "hard to reach" parents who have difficulty in accessing educational opportunities, offers support to all parents at significant stages in their child's development.
- The Emotional Well-being of Children and Young People - supports projects specifically established for the purpose of promoting the emotional well-being of primary school children who are causing concern and promoting the emotional literacy of young people of secondary school age in schools, after-school clubs or youth service settings.
- Out of School Services - assists with the development of out-of-school services and facilities which redress the educational and social disadvantages of children in deprived neighbourhoods in an innovative way.

Arts for Young People includes:

- Pupil Referral Units and In-school Learning Support Units – supports residencies by artists or companies in these units and with the costs of evaluating the initiatives.
- Access to Cultural Venues - provides assistance towards new incentives that help teenagers become familiar with, and enjoy, cultural venues within their locality.

Preference will be given to projects that attempt to share the example of their work with others, which should be indicated in the application.

Social Welfare (Director, Paula Ridley)
The programme will strongly focus on capacity building in local groups and neighbourhoods and those projects which explore new forms of area management and service delivery in both urban and rural areas.

Priority will be given to community groups which are developing new responses to neighbourhood and area regeneration, including new strategies for service delivery and social enterprise, and to communities and professionals working together to develop effective skills and capacity building in any of the following areas: neighbourhood management, housing management, neighbourhood services, health, crime, education and employment.

The programme will also consider research which contributes to explaining and developing knowledge of new policy options to reduce social exclusion.

Grants

244 grants were awarded in 2001 totalling £2,327,888. Grants ranged from £1,000 to £30,000.
2 grants were awarded in the North East
- The Total Learning Challenge (North East) – £10,000
- North East Post Adoption Service - £1,124
FINE has a full list of all grants made.

Applications

Apply in writing to the UK Branch at the address shown, not by telephone, e-mail nor in person.

Calouste Gulbenkian Foundation (Cont..)

The Foundation does not use an application form, nor does it ask for any specified format or length, though succinctness is welcomed. Certain information, however, should be included:

- The exact purpose for which the grant is sought and what difference a grant from the Foundation would make, if successful.
- The amount required, with details of how that budget has been arrived at.
- Information about other sources of income, if any, those that are firm commitments as well as those you are exploring.
- Information about the aims and functions of your organisation and about its legal status. The Foundation sometimes makes a grant available to an organisation which does not yet have charitable status through an organisation which does, when there is a suitable association between them. Please consult the Foundation.
- Your last annual report and any available audited accounts.
- Your plans for monitoring and evaluating the work.

Preliminary work on an application may involve consultation, modification or development and often an on-site visit, all of which takes time. Fully prepared proposals are then considered at the Trustees meetings, though the papers have to be finalised six weeks before each meeting. Approximately the same amount of money is distributed in grants at each meeting.

Exclusions

The Foundation only gives grants to proposals of a charitable kind, usually from organisations which should normally be registered charities or otherwise tax-exempt.
Grants are **not** given for:

- The education, training fees, maintenance or medical costs of individuals.
- The purchase, construction, repair or furnishing of buildings.
- Performances, exhibitions or festivals.
- Conferences or seminars.
- University or similar research.
- Science.
- Medicine or related therapies.
- Holidays of any sort.
- Religious activities.
- Establishing funds for scholarships or loans.
- Projects concerning drug-abuse or alcoholism.
- Animal welfare.
- Sports.
- Equipment, including vehicles or musical instruments.
- Stage, film or television production costs.
- Commercial publications.
- Basic services or core costs (as opposed to imaginative new projects).
- Overseas travel, conference attendance or exchanges.
- Housing.

The Foundation never makes loans or retrospective grants, nor helps to pay off deficits or loans, nor can remedy the withdrawal of statutory funding. Grants are not given in response to any large capital, endowment or widely distributed appeal.

The Camelot Foundation

Correspondent	Julie Gilson Grants Manager 11-13 Lower Grosvenor Place London SW1W 0EX
Telephone	020 7828 6085
Fax	020 7828 6087
E-mail	info@camelotfoundation.org.uk
Website	www.camelotfoundation.org.uk
CC No	1060606
Income	£2,600,00 (2002/03)
Grants	£215,000 (2002/03)
Trustees	D Bryan, F Hasler, R McGowan, D Renshaw, S Slipman OBE, A Spackman OBE, C Pickering, J Graham, N Wragg, D Thompson
Area	UK
Meets	Four times a year

Policy

During April 2002 the Camelot Foundation launched its new strategy for the period 2002-2007. At the heart of its work will be young people who have slipped out of the mainstream of society, or are in danger of doing so. The following four groups will be at the heart of all the Foundation's programmes:

> Young parents, or those at risk of becoming young parents
> Young asylum seekers

- Young people will mental health problems
- Young disabled people

The Foundation's approach is distinctive in three key ways:

- It is committed to a strategy of interconnected programmes, designed to complement each in a way that creates impact far beyond the sheer monetary value of the grants.
- They place a high priority on learning the lessons from the work that they fund. An emphasis on sharing learning is a hallmark of its approach across the programmes.
- They are committed to using all resources – money, knowledge, networks and people – to make an impact in their chosen fields.

The Programmes:
The main funding programme, the Transforming Lives will spend £1 million each year to support the development of new approaches and creative ideas for re-connecting marginalized young people to the mainstream of UK life. Grants between £10,000 and £90,000 are available to registered charities for their work. Detailed grant guidelines and an application form for the Transforming Lives Programme are available from the Foundation.

From 2003 onwards the Annual Leadership Awards will aim to develop skills, broaden thinking and encourage leadership capacity in organisations led by young people.

From 2003 onwards the Strategic Change Programme will provide an opportunity for the Foundation to use the learning from their work to create targeted funding programmes.

The Camelot Foundation (Cont..)

These annual programmes take different forms –

- Take an innovation that has worked well on a small scale and see if the Foundation can allow it to grow it to the next stage of development;
- Identify an issue that appears again and again in applications to the Transforming Lives programme and create a grants programme to tackle that issue;
- Identify a particularly difficult or controversial issue affecting priority groups and design a programme to open up discussion and debate.

Grants
2002 – Round 1
77 applications were received – 3 grants were awarded totalling £215,000.

One was made in the North East of England to The Children's Foundation. A grant of £35,681 to support the Golden Freeway project, which uses web-based "portal technology" to enable young people with cerebral palsy to access specialised information and support their transition from adolescence to independent adulthood. The Children's Foundation is based in Newcastle and the project will work throughout the North East of England.

Applications
For guidelines and project proposal form send SAE (A4) to the value of 33p. Different formats, large print and audiotape available.

Decisions usually take 3 months.

Exclusions
- Work with children under 11 or over 25

- Well- established or routine approaches
- Large national charities, which have an established funding base
- Projects where funding from local or national government has run out
- Work that is responsibility of a local health authority
- Capital projects (buildings)
- Academic research that is not linked to a development project
- Overseas travel
- Play schemes, holidays or after school clubs
- Individuals
- General appeals.

CDENT Environment and Waste Fund

Correspondent: County Durham
Foundation
Jordan House
Finchale Road
Durham
DH1 5HL

Tel: 0191 383 0055

Fax: 0191 383 2969

Email:
cdf@freenet.co.uk

Trustees: G Doubleday, R Harbottle, D Ross, L Rutherford, J Taylor, J Topping, J Wearmouth

Income: No information available

Grants: No information available

Area: Co Durham, Darlington, Sunderland

Meets: No information provided

Policy
County Durham Environmental Trust (CDENT) was formed in 1997 to benefit the environment by encouraging the use of the National Landfill Tax Credit Scheme.

The CDENT Environment and Waste Fund uses donations from Durham County Waste Management Company and aims to support and encourage community and voluntary based organisations to improve their local environment.

The aim of the Fund is to support small scale community schemes which would otherwise not proceed.

Printed guidelines detailing the application criteria are available from the correspondent. The Fund will support a wide range of community environmental projects including landscaping, planting, cleaning up an area of community land, waste reduction or sustainable waste management schemes.

The Fund is administered on behalf of CDENT by the County Durham Foundation.

Grants
Grants of between £500 and £2,500 are available. Only in exceptional circumstances will a larger grant be awarded.

Examples of grants previously awarded include;
- Consett Acorn Trust - £2,250 to set up a school can collection scheme in Derwentside.
- Trimdon Village Hall - £800 to improve a garden adjacent to their community building.

Applications
Guidelines and application forms are available from the correspondent.

Applications are welcome from all community and voluntary organisations which have a constitution. Parish Councils may also apply for projects that fit the criteria.

Exclusions
The Fund **does not** support the following:
- Contributions to large appeals

CDENT Environment and Waste Fund (Cont..)

- Groups with significant uncommitted reserves
- Individuals
- Projects on a site not open to the general public at most times
- Projects outside the area of benefit
- Projects that would normally be
- Undertaken by the local authority or similar body, including work on designated footpaths or highways
- Retrospective or deficit funding
- Sponsored events.

Century Radio Charitable Trust

Correspondent	Jane Spooner Secretary Century House PO Box 100 Church Street Gateshead NE8 2YY
Telephone	0191 477 6666
Fax	0191 478 3509
Email	jane.spooner@centuryfm.co.uk
CC No	1074635
Income	£30,119 (April 2001)
Grants	No information available
Trustees	J Stevenson, J Kenyon, J O'Brian
Area	North East England
Meets	No information available

Policy
The Trust did not respond to requests for information therefore the entry is based upon information previously held by FINE and additional research.

The Trust gives to a wide variety of organisations and projects.

Grants
No information was available.

Applications
In writing to the correspondent.

Century Radio Charitable Trust (Cont..)

Exclusions

The Trust will **not** usually consider grants for the following:

- Individuals and major fundraising appeals
- Major, national fund-raising appeals
- On-going expenses (e.g. rent, telephone, petrol)
- More than one application per year

Helpful Hint...

Try to accentuate the positive and not dwell on the negative things that could happen if the project isn't funded.

Charities Aid Foundation

Correspondent:	The Grants Team Kings Hill West Malling Kent ME19 4TA
Telephone:	01732 520 334
Fax:	01732 520 001
Email:	grants@CAFonline.org
Website:	www.cafonline.org
CC No.	268369
Income:	£1 million (2002)
Grants:	No information given
Trustees:	Advisory Council Members, K Laverby, J Barteman, Y Chauham, G Crosby, Prof. D Landon, J Stock
Area:	United Kingdom
Meets:	various

Policy

The Foundation did not respond to requests for information. The entry is based upon details which appear on the website. The present grants policy seems likely to change in the spring of 2003. At the time of going to print no information was available as to the extent of the policy changes.

The overall aim of Charities Aid Foundation (CAF) is "to enable charities to achieve their purposes more effectively" in order to strengthen the voluntary sector.

Charities Aid Foundation (Cont..)

The aim of the current programme is to build the capacity of charitable organisations by improving their finances, governance and infrastructure.

Applications will be considered from any UK organisation, set up exclusively for charitable purposes, whose annual income does not exceed £1.5 million. Priority will be given to small organisations, with some funds specifically targeted at organisations with an annual income of up to £50,000.

At present there are five funds:

Collaborative Fund
CAF wishes to work in partnership with up to 3 organisations a year. Priority will be given to support the development of their financial, planning and governance structures. Up to £60,000 will be available for one to three years funding.

Consultancy Fund
To support small to medium sized charitable organisations by providing low cost, high quality consultancy and capacity building support.
A consultancy will be offered with CAF Consulting and Development based on the information provided by organisations in their application forms. Organisations will be offered a choice of consultants with CAF funding up to 100% of the costs of the consultancy.

Fast Track Fund
The programme supports organisations that wish to develop and expand nand are seeking immediate funding for specific training needs. The focus of the training must be on strengthening the organisation such as financial management, fundraising,

volunteers or management committee members.
The maximum grant available will be £600.

Minority Ethnic Fund
The fund will support organisations which;
• Are managed by and delivering services to people from communities that are discriminated or disadvantaged because of their race, ethnic or national origin, religion or lifestyle. This is a broad definition and includes jewish and irish communities, travellers, refugees and faith groups.
• Have an annual income of up to £50,000

The maximum grant is £4,000, with the average being around £2,000. The priorities of the fund are to strengthen an organisation's infrastructure. In previous years CAF has funded, development of policies and procedures, strategic and business planning, fundraising strategy, support and training to implement Quality Standards, roles and responsibilities of management committees, project management, financial management and team building.

Short-Term Assistance Fund
Aimed at supporting organisations which are facing short-term financial difficulties due to unforeseen cuts in funding. Organisations need to demonstrate that any one off funding will mean the organisation can plan for the longer term. Applications will be considered from any organisation with an annual turnover of up to £1.5 million, although priority will be given to small organisations. Grants can be for up to £10,000.
The fund will support;
• Existing staff salaries
• General running costs

Charities Aid Foundation (Cont..)

- Up to six months funding
- Rent

Grants

No up to date grants information was available. However in previous years grants made to organisations in the North East have included:

- Age Concern, Gateshead — to provide information to ethnic minority elders
- Alzheimer's Society, Newcastle — to improve accountancy systems and train staff
- Calvert Trust, Kielder - towards the salary of a community fundraiser
- Children's Warehouse, Newcastle — towards consultancy fees for fundraising and business planning
- Northumbria Coalition Against Crime — to develop a corporate fundraising strategy.

Grants should be used within 12 months of receipt.

Applications

All applications must be submitted on an application form which can be obtained from the correspondent or downloaded from the website.

Completed application forms should be returned along with two copies of your governing document, two copies of the most recent financial statement, audited accounts or independently examined accounts, two copies of the most recent annual report and list of management committee members / trustees if not included in the annual report.

Some of the funds require additional information which is listed on the application form.

If you are not a registered charity you must complete an eligibility form and submit it with the application.

Exclusions

In general no grants will be given for the following;

- Start up costs for a new charity
- New initiatives
- Capital items including computers, office equipment, vehicles and refurbishment
- Spending that has already taken place
- Clearing debts or repaying loans
- The erection, repair or purchase of buildings, nor the provision of furniture
- General appeals.

Some of the funds have their own specific exclusions, please check the guidelines.

Helpful Hint...

Submit a well-justified budget that includes income as well as expenditure. But be realistic and don't under-bid. You need to have precise quotes of costs of everything you are asking for.

Chase Charity

Correspondent	Ailsa Hollond
	Secretary
	2 The Court
	High Street
	Harwell
	Didcot
	Oxfordshire
	OX11 0EY
Telephone	01235 820 044

Website
www.chase-charity.org.uk

CC No	207108
Income	£490,714 (2000/01)
Grants	£311,930 (2000/01)
Trustees	G Halcrow, E Moore, N Perry, A Stannard, D Carter, P Curno, S Robertson
Area	UK, except Greater London area and Northern Ireland
Meets	Quarterly

Policy

The Trust supports registered charities which develop community initiatives to meet local needs. They concentrate on smaller charities, many of which will have only a local or regional remit. The Trustees, in particular, support projects which can show evidence of user involvement as well as the proper use and support of volunteers.

The minimum grant is £1,000 and grants are always made for specific purposes, although occasionally revenue funding is supported up to a maximum of three years. Larger grants, up to a maximum of £30,000 are made in the fields of Arts and Heritage.

The Trust has three areas of interest:

Arts
Applications will be considered for work in every aspect of the arts, including community arts and arts centres. The Trustees are particularly interested in helping charities to take their work to communities and groups who would not normally have access to the arts, such as people living in rural areas or those disadvantaged by disability, poverty or age.

Heritage
Applications will be considered for:
- The repair of rural parish churches. The building must be Grade 1 listed in a village of fewer than 500 people and the appeal must be supported by the local community. Grants range from £1,000 to £3,000
- Buildings and artefacts of architectural merit and historical interest, which must be used and be accessible to the community. Priority will be given to rural areas
- Almshouses of architectural merit and historical interest in rural areas.

Social welfare
This is an important area for the Trust, particularly with regard to projects working with the following groups:
- Elderly people
- Families and children
- Homeless
- Mental health
- Neighbourhood work
- Penal affairs
- Physical and learning disabilities
- Young people.

Chase Charity (Cont..)

Grants
In the year ending 31st March 2001 the Trust made 64 grants totalling £526,480. FINE has a full list of grants. In the North East one grant was made to NTC Touring Theatre Company in Alnwick for £10,000 towards the cost of a touring production.

Applications
The Trust produces a leaflet, "How to Apply for a Grant". Applications should be in writing describing:
- Who you are
- What you do
- Why you are seeking the Trust's help
- How you will measure success
- How much money you need to raise
- How soon you need it
- Who else you have asked for help
- What support you have already attracted.

Accompanying the letter should be:
- Information about the origins and current legal status of the organisation
- A copy of the most recent annual report and full audited accounts
- An itemised income and expenditure budget for the work to be funded
- Equal opportunities policy.

Exclusions
In general terms, the Trustees **do not** support:
- Grants to replace funds that have been withdrawn from statutory sources
- Applications to replace time expired grants from the Community Fund or other Lottery distributors
- Large, widely circulated appeals
- Retrospective funding.

More particularly, the Trust does not make grants in support of:
- Adaptations to improve access to buildings
- Advancement of religion
- Animal welfare
- Conferences or seminars
- Endowment funds
- Festivals
- Hospices
- Individuals
- Individual youth clubs
- Large capital projects
- Medical research
- Other grant making bodies
- Publications, films or videos
- Sport
- Schools for people with special needs
- Travel, expeditions or holidays
- Vehicles
- Formal education including institutes of further or higher education, NHS hospital trusts and appeals from associated charities concerned with medical projects.

The Children's Foundation – Regional Small Grants

Correspondent	The Chief Executive The Regional Small Grants Programme PO Box 2YB Queen Victoria Road Newcastle upon Tyne NE99 2YB
Telephone	0191 202 3000
Fax	0191 202 3049
E-mail	childrens.foundation@ncl.ac.uk
Website	www.thechildrensfoundation.co.uk
CC No	1000013
Grants	£10,000 - £25,000 (figure reviewed annually)
Trustees	L Winskill, Prof. K Bartlett, Dr A Cant, S Chapman, Prof. A Craft, Dr J Elliott, J Gill, N Hope, P Judge, G Ross, I Wilson
Area	Northumberland, Tyne & Wear, County Durham and Teesside
Meets	Three times a year, usually in March, July and November

Policy

Regional Small Grants Programme. Funding is generated through the Foundation's Yellow Brick Road Appeal. Any non-profit group which is properly constituted can apply. The programme supports projects which complement and enhance the existing work of The Children's Foundation and which represent "key challenges facing the region", these include: child safety, good parenting, mental health and well-being and physical disability. Grants for equipment for health projects that will not be funded by the NHS will be considered.

Grants

(Awards will be for approximately £1,000).
Previous grant holders include:

- Spennymoor Youth & Community Association, towards transport and specialist equipment hire for children with disabilities - £1,000
- Seaham Youth Centre S.A.N.D.S. Project, for training - £490.43
- Unity Multicultural, Sunderland- to purchase toys for the crèche - £1,000
- Route 26 Community Project, Gateshead- towards a luncheon club - £1,000.

Applications

Application forms are available on request from the Foundation. A copy of your latest accounts must accompany your application.

Exclusions

Grants **cannot** be made for:

- General, non-specific applications
- Grants to individuals
- Holidays
- Items or work that should be funded by health and local authorities
- Repayment of loans
- Revenue costs.

Church Urban Fund

Correspondent	Canon Geoff Miller Co-ordinator Church House St. John's Terrace North Shields NE29 6HS
Telephone	0191 270 4100
Fax	0191 270 4101
E-mail	church_house@newcastle.anglican.org
Website	www.cuf.org.uk
CC No	297483
Income	£2.12 million (2001)
Grants	£2.64 million (2001)
Trustees	The Rt. Rev. J Austin, P Coldsteam CBE, R Farnell, The Ven. G Gibson, M Cornwall-Jones, M Mockridge, S O'Brien CBE, The Revd. Canon J Stanley OBE, D Stwart
Area	England
Meets	Quarterly (March, June, September, December)

Policy

The Church Urban Fund assists community-based projects that tackle issues of disadvantage, poverty and marginalisation in the poorest areas of England's inner cities and outer estates. It was set up in 1988 in response to "Faith In The City", a Church of England report that drew attention to the increasing levels of poverty in urban areas and to the widening gap between rich and poor. The grants it awards serve as a practical demonstration that the Church as a whole is concerned for, and stands with, the most disadvantaged of our society.

Whilst the Fund is rooted in the Christian faith, grants are not restricted on the basis of religious belief. In carrying out its commitment to the teachings of Christ to "love your neighbour as yourself", the Fund recognises the importance of forming partnerships with ecumenical and interfaith projects.

The Fund believes that it can make the most effective use of its limited resources by targeting funds to projects that:
- Are based in an urban priority area, as defined by the Fund
- Involve the local community in identifying needs, initiating responses and running the project
- Are part of the local Anglican Church's outreach to the community or are building working relationships with the Church
- Have charitable purposes
- Are able to raise part of the required money from other sources

Projects that do not meet these minimum criteria are not eligible for funding.

Grants may be awarded for both revenue and capital projects. Grants can be up to £50,000, but do not normally exceed £30,000 in total. Funding from other sources will always be required - a grant from the Fund may be up to 90% of the overall project cost, however the typical level is 30 - 40%, with additional funds required to be raised locally and from other funders.

Church Urban Fund (Cont..)

Small grants of up to £2,000 are available to enable specific small initiatives, such as children's activities or credit union start-ups, or to provide project support such as feasibility studies.

Grants

Grants made by the Church Urban Fund up to the end of July 2002 include:
- Belmont Church and Community Worker, Walker - £27,000 over 3 years
- Contact School Liaison Project, West Newcastle - £25,000 over 3 years
- Denton 2000 Project - £1,500 over one year
- St. Paul's Community Project, Willington Quay- £18,000 over 3 years
- Stepney Bank Stables (Horse Project), Byker - £15,000 over 3 years
- West End Refugee Service (small grant) - £500

Applications

Applicants should contact their local Diocesan Project Co-ordinator for advice on the local procedures for applying. All applications must be supported by the Diocesan Bishop. In considering applications, the Fund will particularly want to know how your project will make a difference and why you think it will succeed. How, should include the types of service or facilities you will offer. Why, should include the strengths of the project, qualifications of staff and volunteers, management structure, assurance of further funding and plans to actively involve users in all stages of the project.

If your applications involves the employment of a worker, the Fund will want to make sure that you have considered the following points:
- Potential increases in salary and employment costs
- Equal opportunities policy
- Job description
- Contract of employment
- Clear management structures and support.

The Fund may support the employment of staff for up to 5 years, but the initial grant will cover a 3 year period. A further application for continuation funding will be required from organisations seeking to extend the 3 year period. Such applications must be supported by a written evaluation of the project, undertaken by an independent body with knowledge of the voluntary and charitable sector.

Applications for revenue funding must be supported by:
- Documentary evidence of the points above, where the application involves the employment of a worker
- The latest annual report and audited accounts of the applicant organisation
- Information about future funding plans.

Applications for capital funding must be supported by:
- A feasibility study, where major capital works are required
- The latest annual report and audited accounts of the applicant organisation
- Information about future funding plans.

Church Urban Fund (Cont..)

Exclusions
Applicants should check that their application will fall within the criteria given above under Policy. The Fund **will not** award grants for:
- Projects outside England
- Individuals
- Clergy stipends
- Work previously funded by a statutory agency that has
- Ceased because of cut-backs, or activities that should be funded by such sources
- Projects based in schools which benefit only that school, or which address basic education needs or other services that should be the responsibility of the local education authority or the school itself
- Voluntary-aided schools eligible for statutory funding
- Direct support to other grant-giving bodies
- Research
- General appeals.

De Clermont Charitable Company Limited

Correspondent	Mrs E K De Clermont Secretary Morris Hall Norham Berwick upon Tweed Northumberland TD15 2JY
CC No	274191
Telephone	01289 382 259
Income	£38,049 (2000/01)
Grants	£24,534 (1996/97)
Trustees	Mrs E K De Clermont, S Orpwood
Area	UK with a preference for the North East of England
Meets	The Trustees respond to appeals as they are received.

Policy
No updated information was received from the Trust; the entry is based upon information previously held by FINE and that which appears on the Charity Commission database.

This Trust gives a very large number of small grants, with some preference for the North East of England. The main interests are firstly medical research and secondly organisations connected with children, young people, older people and people with disability and special needs. Charities for ex-servicemen also feature prominently.

De Clermont Charitable Company Limited (Cont...)

Grants
In the year ending 31 March 1997, the trust awarded more than 250 grants, totalling £24,534. Apart from an exceptional grant of £1,500 to Mowden Hall Appeal, the majority of grants were for £50 to £200.

Applications
In writing to the correspondent.

Exclusions
No grants to individuals or to organisations concerned with drug and alcohol abuse.

Cleveland Community Foundation

Correspondent	Kevin J Ryan FCA Director Southlands Business Centre Ormesby Road Middlesbrough TS3 0HB
Telephone	01642 314 200
Fax	01642 313 700
E-mail	office@clevelandfoundation.org.uk
CC No	700568
Income	£895,526 (2000/01)
Grants	£783,550 (2000/01)
Trustees	Sir R Norman OBE, M Stewart OBE, Dr T Gillham, R Sale, J Foster OBE, C Hope, M Houseman, A Kitching, J Ord OBE, P Sole, I Collinson, G Crute, M Fay, R Ladds, K MacNaught, M Scott
Area	The former County of Cleveland
Meets	There are several different funds, each with their own distribution committee. Frequency and dates vary for each fund.

Policy
The Cleveland Community Foundation gives grant support to organisations and groups working to meet a wide

Cleveland Community Foundation (Cont..)

range of community needs, including support for handicapped people, for youth clubs, for talented musicians, for training within voluntary organisations, sports centres, ethnic groups, community partnerships and crime prevention.

Grants
A total of £783,550 was distributed in grants in 2000/02 (an increase of £134,818 on the previous year).

Teesside Youth Development Fund distributed 62 grants, totalling £82,168 to a wide range of organisations working with disadvantaged and disaffected young people.
Grants ranged from £100 to £5,000.

Teesside TEC Distribution Fund distributed 53 grants, totalling £232,826.

The Cleveland Fund distributed 78 grants, totalling £101,126, to a wide range of organisations. Grants ranged from £100 to £5,000.

The Teesside Power Fund distributed 21 grants, totalling £23,255, to groups supporting the residents living in the nine wards in the Teesside Power Station region. Grants ranged from £350 to £2,000.

The Voluntary Sector Management Training Fund awarded 4 grants, totalling £1,530 to voluntary groups for the training of their volunteers. Grants ranged from £250 to £500.

Applications
Guidelines and application forms are available from the Foundation for each of its funds. Staff at the Foundation are happy to help applicants complete the forms, or may telephone or visit to obtain sufficient information before considering the application.

Each application is considered in light of the following factors:
* Is there a real need for the service or project proposed?
* Can the organisation do the job?
* Does the proposal duplicate existing provision?
* What impact would the grant have?
* The financial stability of the organisation
* Possibility of other sources of funding

Decisions are normally made within three months.

Exclusions
Applications are not usually considered for major fundraising appeals or for sponsored events. Each fund has further exclusions – please read the guidelines carefully.

The Coalfields Regeneration Trust

Correspondent	Ms Jen McKevitt, Regeneration Manager, North East The Eco Centre Room 7B Windmill Way Hebburn NE31 1SR
Telephone	0191 428 5550
Freephone	0800 064 85 60
Fax	0191 428 5005

E-mail
jenm@coalfields-regen.org.uk

Website
www.coalfields-regen.org.uk

CC No	1074930
Income	Projected £50m for 2002-2005
Grants	91p in every pound of the Trust's funds is allocated to grants
Trustees	Rt Rev Alan Morgan, Peter McNestry, Peter Fanning, Bill Flanagan OBE, Ken Greenfield, Paula Hay-Plumb, Vernon Jones CBE DL, Hedley Salt CBE DL, Denise Tate, Sylvia Wileman, Joe Wills

Area	Current and former coalfields communities in England, Scotland and Wales
Meets	Every six weeks

Policy

The Coalfields Regeneration Trust is an independent charity, committed to achieving social and economic regeneration in current and former coalfield areas of England, Scotland and Wales.

The Trust is one of the most significant and effective investors in coalfield communities, having funded projects to a total value of over £50m since its launch in 1999.

Far from being "just" a grant-maker, a key feature of the Trust is its ability to offer community groups the advice and support they need to formulate their ideas, and turn them into successful projects. This is achieved through a network of highly-experienced Regeneration Managers and Support Workers, who combine on-the-ground knowledge of local problems, issues and opportunities, with a broader knowledge of community-led regeneration work and funding regimes.

The Trust supports projects within coalfield areas that relate to the following broad themes:

<u>Resourcing and empowering communities</u>.- By helping to develop communities' asset bases, the Trust aims to improve access to facilities, and develop welfare provision and opportunities in coalfield communities. The Trust also works to empower local

The Coalfields Regeneration Trust (Cont..)

people, helping them to take a more active part in the regeneration of their locality.

Encouraging enterprise - The Trust seeks to increase the range, diversity and accessibility of local community enterprises and business start-ups within coalfield areas.

Promoting Lifelong Learning - The Trust helps to provide access to education, skills and other forms of support that help communities to achieve their full potential.

Enhancing environments - Whilst the Trust concentrates on social and economic priorities, it also recognises the need to protect and improve natural and built environments within coalfield areas.

Supporting employment - Employment and access to employment are vital if communities are to achieve economic sustainability. The Trust assists with the delivery of welfare-to-work initiatives that contribute to social inclusion.

Promoting good practice - The Trust is actively involved in identifying projects that demonstrate excellence, creativity and achievement, and in spreading best practice throughout the coalfields, in partnership with other agencies.

A key theme for the Trust over the next three years will be projects which benefit young people, in line with the aims of "Regenerate" - a fundraising campaign that will raise awareness of the issues faced by those aged 26 or under in British coalfield communities.

Grants

In Round One (1999-March 2002) the Trust funded 118 projects in the North-East, to a total value of £7,897,226. A list of grants awarded by the Trust is available on the website. The Round One spend also included strategic partnerships with two Community Foundations and a County Council that enabled the Trust to make over 600 small grants to community groups across Tyne & Wear, County Durham and Northumberland.

Round Two began in April 2002, and will continue until 2005. Examples of Round Two grants include:
• Women's Health Advice Centre (Northumberland) £81,187
• Rekendyke & St Jude PCC (Tyne & Wear) £18,074
• Derwentside CVS & Volunteer Bureau (County Durham) £86,513

Applications

Voluntary and community groups can apply for grants to fund capital or revenue costs, under one of three funding streams:
• Bridging the Gap: a fast-track programme for grants of between £500 and £10,000. The Trust want to ensure that funds are available to those groups which have traditionally had greatest difficulty in attracting funding. Contact Ms Ashleigh Gibson at the correspondent address for further details.
• Small grants: for grants of between £10,000 and £30,000
• Main grants: for grants of £30,000+

There is also an application procedure for statutory bodies.

All applicants are advised to make contact with their nearest Coalfield

The Coalfields Regeneration Trust (Cont..)

Regeneration Trust office prior to making an application, to discuss their project, and the best way forward. The office can provide assistance in completing the official application form.

In addition to grant awards, the Trust is developing a programme of directly-managed projects that tackle coalfields issues in innovative ways. Approaches from organisations who wish to partner the Trust in these strategic interventions are welcomed.

Exclusions

Projects are considered ineligible if they **do not** specifically target coalfields communities, or do not meet the detailed regeneration priorities for each region. The Trust will not fund projects with political or religious objectives. Trust staff can give initial advice on project suitability prior to application.

Comic Relief

Correspondent	Peter Argall UK Grants Manager 5th Floor 89 Albert Embankment London SE1 7TP
Telephone	020 7820 5555
Fax	020 7820 5500
Minicom	020 7820 5579

E-mail
red@comicrelief.org.uk

Website
www.comicrelief.org.uk

CC No	326568
Income	£66,666,443(00/01)
Grants	£19,038,596(00/01)
Trustees	P Bennett-Jones, R Curtis, C Howes, E Freud, M Harris, L Henery, N Varma, L Newman, J K Rowling, A Tucker, M Freud, M Letts, C Lloyd, E Nicoli
Area	UK, Africa and International
Meets	8 times a year

Policy

Comic Relief exists to tackle poverty and social injustice by helping disadvantaged people in the UK, Africa and internationally to realise their potential.

Comic Relief (Cont..)

The main fundraising event, Red Nose Day, takes place every two years. Red Nose Day in March 2001 has raised over £55million. Guidelines and applications are available, covering 2001-2003. The main areas to be funded are as follows:

Supporting Young People
Supports groups providing intensive intervention to young people aged 11 to 25 who are experiencing difficulties in their lives and who are at a point of crisis. Some examples include work around drug and alcohol misuse, homelessness, mental ill health, abuse through prostitution, violence, criminal justice and abuse. Comic Relief also want to fund projects that work with young people to address the whole range of problems they may face.

Fighting for Justice
Supports groups who are challenging the barriers to equal rights and pushing for change so that people are able to participate in society, get their needs met and their voices heard. Comic Relief particularly wants to fund advocacy work, campaigning for better services and work that improves communication between service users and service providers. Applications are welcome from any group pf people facing poverty, disadvantage and discrimination. Some examples include: disabled people, older people, people living with HIV/AIDS, travellers, people experiencing racial harassment, lesbians and gay men and "survivors" of mental health services.

Strengthening Services: the Domestic Violence and Refugee Sectors
Supports the strengthening of the domestic violence and refugee sectors by providing core funding and capacity building grants for individual agencies and by working with both sectors to help secure a better funding environment and help them access statutory sources of funding.

Supporting Communities
Supports a range of self-help projects in deprived communities that are addressing poverty and disadvantage and are putting into practice ideas that local people feel will make a real difference in their communities.

These may be in urban or rural areas. Comic Relief particularly wants to fund groups of people who are active in the communities they live in and are directly affected by the issues they are working to address.

Grants
27 grants were made to North East organisations in 2001 totalling £771,080.25.
Examples include:
- Create Freedom from Sexual Violence (Tees Valley) - £1,445.25
- Consett Churches Detached Youth Project - £22,500
- Disability Outlook (Durham) - £48,000
- Gateshead People - £19,000
- The Outpost Housing Project (Newcastle) - £69,000
- Streetwise (North Tyneside) - £79,658
- Trinity Youth Association (Northumberland) - £45,000

Applications
If you would like to talk to someone before you apply, the staff in the UK Grants Team are happy to discuss your ideas with you.
Please send an A4 Self Addressed Envelope (57p 1st Class Stamp or 31p 2nd Class Stamp) to obtain a copy of the most up to date guidelines (also available in large print, on audio tape and in Braille).

Comic Relief (Cont...)

Grants are available for both running costs (either for core costs or for specific projects) and capital costs (however large capital costs are a low priority).

Small Grants Programme – this is only open to small, local groups with an annual turnover of up to £100,000. The most you can apply for is £5,000 and a priority is given to applications for core and equipment costs. You should have a decision within 3 months.

Large Grants Programme – If you want to apply for more than £5,000, there are two stages to the application process and it may take up to six months to deal with your application. They can give grants for running costs (core costs or project cost) for up to 3 years. There will be five grant-making cycles with the same amount of funding available at each cycle.

Any work funded must be charitable, so if your group is not a registered charity, funds will be paid through a registered charity who then pass the grant on to you.

Exclusions
Comic Relief **do not** fund the following:
- Academic research
- General appeals
- Schools, colleges and hospitals
- Individuals
- Promoting religion
- Trips abroad
- Holidays and outings
- Services run by statutory or public authorities
- Medical research or equipment
- Minibuses
- Sporting activities.

The Community Foundation serving Tyne & Wear and Northumberland

Correspondent	Community Foundation Percy House Percy Street Newcastle upon Tyne NE1 4PW
Telephone	0191 222 0945
Fax	0191 230 0689
E-mail	general@communityfoundation.org.uk
Website	www.communityfoundation.org.uk
CC No	700510
Income	£7,600,000 (01/02)
Grants	£4,600,000 (01/02)
Trustees	S Black MBE, S Brown, P Denham, B Dennis OBE, A Ferguson, Cllr G Gill CBE DL, J Hamilton OBE, J Higginson, R Hollinshead, R McLachlan, J Mowbray, C Parkin, G Readman OBE, C Sinclair, D Smail OBE TD DL, D Walker, T Webb, Hugh Welch, J Worters, M Worthington
Area	Tyne & Wear and Northumberland, occasionally other areas

Community Foundation (Cont...)

Meets   Grants panels and committees meet and award grants throughout the year

Policy

The Community Foundation serving Tyne & Wear and Northumberland provides a service to individuals, families, companies and others who want to help the local community.

The Community Foundation makes grants to a wide variety of projects and organisations including:
- Community Associations, residents' and tenants' associations
- Neighbourhood advice centres
- Community regeneration projects
- Organisations working with older people, encouraging active involvement in their communities
- A wide range of work with children and young people
- Projects tackling homelessness
- Projects run by and for disabled people, people from minority ethnic groups, carers and other minority groups
- Community arts projects and informal education which may or may not be accredited
- Projects which help people to get the necessary skills to get a good job, and / or support them through the process of finding work
- Projects involving women
- Small scale community environmental projects.

Small Grants Programme
Grants are available under the Small Grants Programme for up to £5,000 (from April 2003).
The priorities of the programme are as follows:
- One-off grants that provide practical help

- Grants for training and development for small groups
- Feasibilities and evaluations funded
- Projects that cannot be funded elsewhere
- It will not make small contributions to much larger projects
- Priority to groups in both urban and rural areas where there is evidence of need and disadvantage
- Priority to groups which are locally run and are led by and use volunteers fully

There is no closing date for applications, which will be considered by the Community Foundation Grants Panel every two months, and by donors on a rolling basis. The foundation will normally give a response to applications within three months.

The Community Foundation, in addition to a range of funds held by private and corporate donors, also administers the **Joseph Brough Charitable Trust.**

This gives grants of up to £2,500, occasionally more, to charitable projects with an emphasis on the Methodist Church. Some grants are for small capital projects such as refurbishments. The Trust's area of benefit is the North East region.

Applicants should use the Community Foundation's single application process and will normally receive a decision within three months.

The Community Foundation will prioritise projects which:
- Help people in greatest need
- Involve minority and disadvantaged groups

Community Foundation (Cont..)

- Are locally run and led
- Use volunteers fully
- Help the development of the voluntary sector.

Grants

The Community Foundation under its main grants programme, makes, both one-off and recurrent grants, for up to three years, for capital items, organisation running costs, project revenue costs and to individuals.
The Community Foundation has awarded grants to the following organisations. (These are just a few examples).

- Mediation in North Tyneside – £4,000 for revenue costs
- Berwick Citizens' Advice Bureau - £5,000 to cover a shortfall in running costs
- BRIDGE - £750 funding for a three day residential experience
- Whalton Out of School Club - £750 to equip a new building
- 8th Cramlington Brownie Guides - £300 for safety equipment
- Morpeth and District Credit Union Study Group - £500 towards set-up and registration costs
- Sunderland Kidney Patient Group - £1,000 for the refurbishment of new office premises
- Open Clasp Theatre Company - £1,000 for the cost of 25 shows and workshops

Applications

Guidelines and applications forms are available from the Community Foundation main grants programme. The Foundation welcomes exploratory telephone calls from organisations thinking of applying.
All applications are acknowledged and all applicants, whether successful or unsuccessful, will be informed of the outcome of their application.

The Foundation often makes telephone calls and / or visits to projects and organisations prior to a decision on the application in order to find out more about the application.

There are no formal restrictions for re-applying. The Foundation recommends that successful and unsuccessful applicants enquire before re-applying.

Exclusions

The Community Foundation **does not** make awards for:

- Sponsorship and fundraising events
- Small contributions to major appeals
- Large capital projects
- Endowments
- Political or religious groups
- Work which should be funded by health and local authorities, or government grant aid
- Projects outside the beneficial area

The Community Foundation also administers government funded **Neighbourhood Renewal Community Chests** in collaboration with local development agencies in the five Tyne & Wear districts and the Wansbeck district of Northumberland. Applicants should contact their local development agency – a list is attached to the guidelines. Similarly it runs the **Local Network Fund for children and young people** in Tyne & Wear and Northumberland. Groups should Tel. 0845 113 0161 for an application pack and contact their local development agency for help with project planning, constitutions, filling the form, etc. – the phone numbers are on the attached information sheet. These two funds are provided by the government's Neighbourhood Renewal Unit and Children and Young People's Unit respectively.

Community Foundation (Cont..)

The Community Foundation administers the **TyneWear Partnership Included Communities Fund**. This is part of One North East's Single Programme, and can provide grants for projects from £5,000 to £100,000 to address problems of social and economic exclusion. It will fund projects that work towards enabling the community to become more employable and add to capacity and regeneration initiatives.

Within "Included Communities" groups can apply for projects that focus on:
- Addressing barriers to employment
- Increasing employability
- Enabling the voluntary sector to attract additional resources
- Developing the capacity of the community and voluntary sector to contribute to the renaissance of the North East
- Support the most disadvantaged communities and people in Tyne & Wear.

Finances: -
- There is £450,00 to be allocated within the Included Communities Fund during the financial year to March 31st 2003, and there is likely to be further funding in subsequent financial years.
- The grants can be awarded for capital, revenue, or a combination of the two
- The grants will be made on a one off basis for the financial year, 2002/2003 and must be spent by 31st March 2003
- Match funding is encouraged but they will consider 100% funding.

Continuation Charitable Trust

Correspondent	Mr R B Bradbeer Messrs Eversheds, Solicitors Central Square South Orchard Street Newcastle upon Tyne NE1 3XX
Telephone	0191 241 6000
Fax	0191 241 6499
CC No	279724
Income	No information available
Grants	No information available
Trustees	R B Bradbeer, P J Dudding, C D Legge, R Nicholson
Area	North East of England and the Third World
Meets	Twice a year, in April and October

Policy
The Trustees consider each application on its own merit and look at the viability and competence of the application. Any type of project or charity may be given a donation or grant, but preference is usually given to registered charities. Large, well known charities are generally only supported through their local branches.

Grants
No information supplied.

Continuation Charitable Trust (Cont...)

Applications
Apply in writing to the correspondent. Only successful applications will be acknowledged.

Exclusions
The Trust **does not** make grants to individuals or for private education and will not acknowledge any such application received.

Helpful Hint...

Use headed paper. It should be clear, informative and quote your charity registration number.

Catherine Cookson Charitable Trust

Correspondent:	Peter Magnay Thomas Magnay & Co 13 Regent Terrace Gateshead NE8 1LU
Tel:	0191 488 7459
Fax:	0191 488 8682

Email
whickham@magnay.u-net.com

Trustees:	J E Ravenscroft, W R McBrien, H F Marshall, P Magnay, D S S Hawkins
Income:	£1,945,217 (2000)
Grants:	£737,245 (1999)
Area:	UK and Worldwide
Meets:	No information available

Policy
The Trust did not respond to requests for information, therefore this entry has been compiled from details from the Charity Commission for England and Wales.

There are no written guidelines. Grants are awarded at the discretion of the Trustees and in accordance to the wishes of Catherine Cookson.

Grants are made to support a wide range of activities, including education/training, medical/health/sickness, disability, religious activities, arts/culture and environment/conservation/heritage as

Catherine Cookson Charitable Trust (Cont...)

well as general charitable purposes. In particular the Trust supports work with children and young people, older people and people with a disability or special needs.

In the past grants have been given to statutory bodies, schools, churches, charities and non-registered organisations.

Grants
According to the last published Annual Report and Statement of Accounts 144 grants were made ranging from £250 to £100,000.

Grants given to North East organisations during 1999/2000 included:
- Bede's World - £100,000
- Westoe Methodist Church (South Shields) - £2,000
- Consett Churches Detached Youth Project - £2,000
- Newcastle upon Tyne Dog and Cat Shelter - £2,000
- Friends of Jesmond Dene - £1,000
- Ponteland County Middle School – £1,000
- Denton Burn Community Association - £1,000
- Felling Royals Jazz Band - £1,000
- 1338 Air Training Corp Seaham – £500
- 88 Newcastle Brownies - £500
- Multiple Sclerosis Society - £500
- DLI Museum Appeal - £250
- Tyneside Foyer - £250
- St. Georges Playgroup - £250

Applications
There is no application form. Written applications, enclosing a SAE, should be sent to the correspondent.

Exclusions
No information available.

County Durham Foundation

Correspondent	Gillian Stacey Director Suite 2 Jordan House Forster Business Centre Finchale Road Durham DH1 5HL
Telephone	0191 383 0055
Fax	0191 383 2969
E-mail	info@countydurhamfoundation.co.uk
Website	www.countydurhamfoundation.co.uk
CC No	1047625
Income	£2,570,632(2001)
Grants	£958,350 (2001/02)
Trustees	Sir P Nicholson, P Cook DL, R Wilkinson, H Barrie, D Brown CBE, Professor J Clarke DL, B Keel, J Lund, A MacConachie DL, Lady Nicholson, K Richards, B Robinson OBE DL, D Watson, Mark I'Anson, Frances Bourne, David L Brown, Michele Armstrong, John Fitzpatrick, Hilary Florek, John Hamilton, Mark Lloyd, Judith Lund, Cllr. Robin Todd, Paul Wilding

County Durham Foundation (Cont..)

Area   County Durham and Darlington only (Grants for individuals can be given in the wider area of the North East)

Meets   There are several different funds, each with their own distribution committees. Frequency and dates of meetings vary for each fund.

Policy

County Durham Foundation awards grants to groups that are charitable, educational or benevolent in purpose.

The Foundation mostly fund projects that:
- Meet identified needs or issues in a sustainable way in disadvantaged geographic areas
- Are from groups that are run by local people for local people, and often involve users in their management committee
- Demonstrate community involvement by engaging as many people as possible and ensure that users have a say in how projects are run
- Specifically target disadvantaged communities i.e. work with black and ethnic minority communities, young people, faith groups, travellers, the elderly, people with disabilities and refugees
- Are for new and innovative projects that do not duplicate an existing service already provided locally

- Are run by groups that demonstrate that they have the ability to deliver the proposed project
- Demonstrate real value for money, with a realistic budget.

Priority will be given to applications from those organisations working with (and preferably run by):
- Children and young people
- Young parents
- Faith groups engaged in non-religious community activities
- Local community regeneration partnerships, residents and tenant's associations
- Elderly people
- People with disabilities or health related problems
- Homeless people
- Black and minority ethnic communities
- Rural communities
- Travellers and refugee groups
- Local people interested in small scale environmental improvements or waste recycling or reduction schemes
- Group and community based training and education programmes, particularly those who have previously had no access to training opportunities.

The Community Action Grants programme is funded from County Durham Foundation's endowment fund. The maximum size grant is £400 and the Foundation are particularly looking to fund new groups and projects in Chester le Street, Darlington, Durham City and Teesdale, although groups from other districts can also apply.

The County Durham Foundation also administers the following funds:
- Local Network Fund and Investing in Children

County Durham Foundation (Cont..)

- Community Environment and Community Waste Funds (listed separately in this guide)
- Neighbourhood Renewal Community Chest
- Community Learning Chest.

An organisation can hold one grant from each programme every 12 months.

Grants
Grants are available from £50 to £7,000 from a variety of different grant programmes.

Grants made by the County Durham Foundation during 2001/2002 include:
- Tyne Tees Girls Youth Football Team - £150 towards running costs
- Leadgate Dance Club - £220 towards core costs and a music centre
- Famous Ladies Residents' Association - £1,000 to support a two week playscheme
- West Rainton & Leamside Community Association - £500 for new toys and equipment for Mother and Toddler group
- Carrside Youth Club - £500 to create a website for the club
- Thornley Youth Musical & Social Group - £320 contribution towards the hire and set up of a mixing desk, earphones and lighting for the Thornley Intergenerational Musical Project
- South West Durham Credit Union Study Group - £360 to pay the registration fee of the credit union / financial services authority.

Applications
Application forms and guidelines are available from the Foundation.

Applications will only be accepted on the official form. You must include with your application:
- A copy of your constitution, or if you are a new group a set of rules that explains what you do and how you take decisions
- A full set of examined accounts, or if you are a new group a bank statement plus an annual budget showing estimated income and expenditure, authorised by your Treasurer
- If your project works with children a copy of your Child Protection Policy
- Equal Opportunities Policy.

If your project is an environmental project you must supply:
- the landowners written permission
- detailed plans and sketches for the site, which can be prepared by a landscape architect
- photographs of the proposed site.

You must also have a bank or building society account which requires at least two unrelated signatories. If you do not have a bank or building society account, you can nominate a recognised group, such as a local Council for Voluntary Service (CVS) to receive the grants on your behalf.

Exclusions
The County Durham Foundation **do not** fund the following:
- Groups that have substantial free reserves (over £15,000) or are in serious deficit
- National charities that have no local office
- Projects outside County Durham and Darlington (groups from Sunderland can apply for environmental grants)
- A contribution towards large projects (with a total budget of over £10,000)
- Grants for more than one year

County Durham Foundation (Cont..)

- General appeals
- Individuals (alternative grants are available for individuals)
- General appeals, sponsorship and marketing appeals
- Membership applications
- Expeditions and overseas travel
- Minibuses or other vehicle purchases
- Holidays
- Endowments, loans or guarantee bonds
- Deficit or retrospective funding
- Replacement of statutory funding / responsibilities, including work on designated footpaths or highways i.e. roundabouts and verges
- Excessive overheads
- Lap-top computers (unless for people with special needs)
- Political, exclusively religious activities or funding for the promotion of religion
- Animal welfare
- Mainstream education including Parents and Teachers Associations that do not have a strong community involvement (schools can apply for environmental projects)
- Development of any land that is not open to the general public at convenient hours
- Medical research, hospitals or medical centres
- Building or buying premises, or freehold or leasehold land rights
- Unpaid or contingent liabilities, bad debts, fines or interest charges
- Service charges for finance leases, hire purchase or credit arrangements
- Depreciation of fixed assets.

Lord Crewe's Charity

Correspondent	David Palfrey Dean & Chapter of Durham The College Durham DH1 3EH
Telephone	0191 386 4266
Email	david.palfrey@durhamcathedral.co.uk
CC No	230347
Income	£594,522 (2001)
Grants	No information given
Trustees	Ven. G G Gibson, Ven. T Willmott, Ven. P Elliott, Hon. H Vine, J Brown-Swinburne, W F P Hugonin, Rector of Lincoln College Oxford
Area	Dioceses of Newcastle and Durham
Meets	May and November

Policy
The Charity did not provide up to date information. The entry is based upon information held on the Charity Commission database and additional FINE research.

The Charity provides grants for the following:
- The repair or construction of churches, chancels and parsonages within the area of benefit
- The support of needy clergy and their dependents

Lord Crewe's Charity (Cont...)

- Organisations which have charitable purposes and benefit the residents living within the area of benefit, particularly the relief of poverty.

Grants
No information available.

Applications
Application forms are available from the correspondent.

Exclusions
Organisations outside the Dioceses of Newcastle and Durham.

Cumberland Building Society Charitable Foundation

Correspondent	Mrs J A Thomson Secretary to the Trustees Cumberland House Castle Street Carlisle Cumbria CA3 8RX
Telephone	01228 541341
Fax	01228 403111

E-mail
executives@cumberland.co.uk

Website
www.cumberland.co.uk

CC No	1072435
Income	£146,892 (2001)
Grants	£33,600 (2001/02)
Trustees	Mr J G Gaddes, Mrs H Irving, Mr M J Shannon, Mr J G Stewart, Mr R Wilkinson
Area	Cumbria, Dumfriesshire, Lancashire (Preston area) and Northumberland (Haltwhistle area)
Meets	Quarterly

Policy
The Foundation makes grants of between £250 and £1,000 to registered charities. Requests for donations will be considered from

Cumberland Building Society Charitable Foundation (Cont...)

organisations which appear to the Trustees to be for the benefit of persons resident in, or otherwise connected with, the society's operating area of Cumbria, Dumfriesshire, Lancashire (Preston area) and Northumberland (Haltwhistle area). Requests for donations from the same charity will only be considered once in any 12 month period.

Grants
No information available.

Applications
The Foundation does not use an application form and does not produce guidelines, however exploratory telephone calls are welcome. Application is in writing to the correspondent.

The Foundation occasionally telephones applicants for further information regarding their application. All applications are acknowledged and all applicants, whether successful or unsuccessful, will be contacted.

Exclusions
None supplied.

Hedley Denton Charitable Trust

Correspondent	Ian Nicholson Chairman of Trustees 5 West Road Ponteland Newcastle upon Tyne NE20 9ST
Telephone	01661 823863
Fax	01661 823724
E mail	law@iannicholson.co.uk
CC No	1060725
Income	£40,000 (2002)
Grants	£37,000 (2002)
Trustees	I Nicholson, D Wild, C Watts
Area	Mainly North East England
Meets	Twice a year

Policy
The Trust makes one-off grants, ranging from £500 to £7,000, to Registered Charities. The following areas of work normally fall within the Trust's policy:
• Arts / Culture
• Carers
• Children / Young People
• Community Care
• Conservation of Buildings (including Churches)
• Disadvantaged / Poverty
• Education / Training
• Elderly
• Employment Training / Unemployed

Hedley Denton Charitable Trust (Cont..)

- Environment / Nature Conservation
- Health and Medicine
- Homeless / Housing
- Hospitals / Hospices
- International
- Mental Health
- General Charitable Purposes

The Trust will award grants to support:
- Capital items
- Organisation running costs
- Building work
- Project revenue costs

Grants
Grants awarded range between £500 and £2,000.

Applications
Written applications only.
Successful applicants are required to wait for 12 months before re-applying. It is not generally worthwhile for unsuccessful applicants to re-apply.

Exclusions
No information given.

Diana, Princess of Wales Memorial Fund

Correspondent	Grants Department (UK) The County Hall Westminster Bridge Road London SE1 7PB
Telephone	020 7902 5500
Website	www.theworkcontinues.org
CC No	1064238
Income	£5,740,000 (2001)
Grants	No information given
Area	UK and international
Meets	Twice a year

Policy
The criteria for the grants programme is reviewed yearly around December time. It is envisaged that the theme for 2003 will broadly remain unchanged to that of 2002, that is, helping young people in the transition to adulthood and independence. Any organisation wishing to apply is requested to obtain the most up to date guidelines before submitting an application. These can be obtained from the correspondent or downloaded from the website.

The Fund will support organisations working with children and young people between the ages of 12 and 25.

Support will only be given to work that is of a national significance. This means work that is good practice that can be applied in other areas of the UK

Diana, Princess of Wales Memorial Fund (Cont..)

and takes a new approach to an issue or has a particular strategic significance in the development of an area of work.

Organisations do not need to be national organisations and projects in rural and inner-city areas can be nationally significant.

At present funding will be given under the following categories:
Refugees and asylum seekers –
particularly work involving:
- Specialist youth work
- Culturally appropriate advice and counselling
- Support for young people and their families
- The development of refugee community organisations in the dispersal areas
- The development of networks between refugee community organisations
- The inclusion of young refugees and asylum seekers into mainstream voluntary sector provision.

Prisoners' Families
Applications will be considered for:
- Work with young people with a family member in prison
- Young people in the penal system who are parents and their partners
- Family members bringing up the child of a young person in prison.

Young People and mental health
Eligible projects include those working with:
- Young people who are most at risk of developing mental illness
- Young people who self harm
- Young men
- Young single mothers
- Young people with non-custodial sentences, those in the penal

system and those leaving the penal system
- Young people from black and minority ethnic communities.

Young people with learning difficulties
Organisations working with young people with a specific physical disability that creates a barrier to learning are not eligible for funding. The fund is very specific about its definition of learning disability and applicants are requested to consult the guidelines.

Advocacy, campaigning and awareness raising
Work must be directly related to one of the aforementioned categories. The following types of advocacy will be considered for funding:
- Self advocacy
- Citizen advocacy
- Crisis advocacy
- Peer advocacy.

Action research and pilot projects / extension of existing categories
The Fund will consider action research and pilot projects for work that is innovative, strategic or deals with a particularly marginalised group in the following categories:
- Young people in the penal system
- Young single parents.

Grants
No specific grant range information was available, but as a guideline, the Fund made the following grants in 2001;
- £60,000 to a young peoples theatre group to work with young people from refugee communities;
- £298,500 for a mental health project to support young learning disabled people, covering a wide range of issues such as human rights and social and life skills;

Diana, Princess of Wales Memorial Fund (Cont..)

- £49,490 to a youth organisation to focus on young prisoners who are parents and collect first hand material regarding their experiences and difficulties in parenting in order to produce a handbook to assist other young prisoners and their families.

Applications
Application packs and criteria are available from the correspondent. To receive an application pack, please send an A4 stamped (84p) self addressed envelope.
Provisional closing dates for applications in 2003 are March 2003 and July 2003.

Exclusions
Work that is a statutory responsibility.

Dickon Trust

Correspondent	Helen Tavroges St. Anns Wharf 112 Quayside Newcastle upon Tyne NE99 1SB
Telephone	0191 279 9000
Fax	0191 279 9100
CC No	326687
Income	£44,663 (2000/01)
Grants	£27,000 (1998/99)
Trustees	J R Barrett, Mrs D L Barrett, P J Dudding, Brigadier R V Brims, R R V Nicholson
Area	Mainly in the North East of England, particularly Northumberland
Meets	No information given

Policy
No updated information was received from the Trust; the entry is based upon information previously held by FINE and that which appears on the Charity Commission database.

Set up in 1986, the Trust provides grants to a wide range of organisations which have charitable purposes, but particularly those benefiting children.

Grants
The Trust awarded grants totalling £27,000 in 1998/99, including the following:
- Northumberland Association of Boys Clubs - £1,000

Dickon Trust (Cont...)

- Red Cross (Northumbria Branch) - £1,000
- Hexham Primary School - £500
- Holy Trinity Church, Berwick - £250

Applications
In writing to the correspondent.

Exclusions
No information given.

Helpful Hint...

Follow the application procedure and always honour the funder's preference with respect to phone or written enquiries.

Exclusive Charity Haggerston Owners (ECHO)

Correspondent	Sean Quilty Secretary The Owners Lounge Haggerston Castle Holiday Park Beal Berwick upon Tweed Northumberland TD15 2PA
Telephone	01289 381 419
Fax	01289 381 337
E-mail	sean.quilty@bourne-leisure.co.uk
CC No	1064455
Income	£13,000 (2001)
Grants	£12,000 (2001)
Trustees	Joan Mason, Heather Davidson
Area	North East and Scotland
Meets	Last Sunday of the months between March and October

Policy
ECHO make one-off grants of up to £2,000. The focus of the Charity is on the provision of equipment to groups working with or for the following:
- Carers
- Children / Young People
- Community Care
- Community Development
- Counselling
- Disabilities
- Family life / Welfare
- Health / Medicine

Exclusive Charity Haggerston Owners (Cont...)

- Hospices / Hospitals
- Mental Health
- Recreation / Leisure / Sport
- Social Welfare

Grants
During 2001 13 grants were made, totalling £12,000.

Applications
Application is in writing to the correspondent. Your application letter should include:
- Information about your organisation
- What the benefit of the equipment would be
- Who would benefit from the purchase
- How many people would benefit
- Equipment required
- Function of the equipment
- Cost of the equipment
- Details of the supplier of the equipment

All applications are acknowledged. Successful and unsuccessful applicants will be contacted.

Successful applicants should wait a minimum of 5 years before re-applying. Unsuccessful applicants may re-apply after 2 years.

Exclusions
None supplied.

Esmée Fairbairn Foundation

Correspondent	Margaret Hyde Director 11 Park Place London SW1A 1LP
Telephone	020 7297 4700
Fax	020 7297 4701
E-mail	info@esmeefairbairn.org.uk
Website	www.esmessfairbairn.org.uk
CC No	200051
Income	£31,918,000 (2001)
Grants	£24,894,000 (2001)
Trustees	J S Fairbairn, J Hardie CBE, Sir A Acland KG, A G Down, Felicity Fairbairn, P Hughes-Hallett, R Kent, K Lampard, M L Fox, Baroness Linklater, Lord Rees-Mogg, W Seighart
Area	UK

Policy
The Foundation makes grants under four sectors, these are:
- Arts and Heritage
- Education
- Environment
- Social Development

Within each of these sectors of interest the Foundation gives priority to applications dealing with particular needs or types of activity – please get

Esmée Fairbairn Foundation (Cont..)

hold of up to date guidelines for further details.

In general, the Foundation favours projects which will contribute to the preservation and development of a free and stable society, with preference for projects which are innovative, developmental, designed to make a practical impact on a particular problem or area of need and reflect the principles of market forces.

Especially in the case of local projects, preference is given to those which demonstrate active local participation and support self help.

The Foundation's area of interest is UK-wide, however the Trustees aim to give particular attention to the less advantaged areas. The Foundation will consider applications from registered charities and groups with charitable purposes. Applications from black and minority ethnic groups are welcomed and the Foundation will be alert to the needs of disabled people in all appropriate funding decisions.

The Foundation attaches importance to the assessment and dissemination of the results of work it has funded, so that others may benefit.

Grants range from £500 to £500,000 and may be made towards revenue or project expenditure, either one year or phased. There is no set pattern for making grants up to a specific percentage of the cost of a project and, in certain circumstances, grants up to 100% may be considered, although the Foundation looks favourably on projects undertaken in partnership, e.g. with another charitable trust.

Even if a project fits the Foundation's policy priorities, it may not be possible to make a grant, as the Foundation receives many more applications than it has funds to support.

Grants
The Foundation awarded grants totalling £24,894,000 in 2001.

The breakdown by sector of the grants awarded during 2001 was:
- Arts & heritage   £5,451,000
- Education   £5,220,000
- Environment   £4,532,000
- Social Development   £9,527,000

There were shared grants to the value of £559,000 awarded.

The North East of England received 46.7pence per head of the population in grants in 2001.

The following is a selection of those awarded in North East England.
- Advocacy in Gateshead - £22,014. Towards the salary of a Self-Advocacy Worker to provide services for adults with learning disabilities
- 2D Support for the Voluntary and Community Sector of Teesside - £39,000. Towards the salary of a part-time Volunteer Co-ordinator over three years
- Berwick Youth Project – £75,000. Towards the salary of the Project Manager providing welfare services to 14 – 25 year olds
- Pennywell Youth Project - £44,461. Towards the core costs and salaries of a Project Manager and a Modern Apprentice to work with schools and the police to provide disadvantaged young people with the opportunities to gain new skills
- Blyth Detached Project - £6,000

Esmée Fairbairn Foundation (Cont..)

- Botanic Centre Middlesbrough - £72,300. Towards the costs of the Wildflower Ark project which maintains plant databases and develops activities for schools and the local community in order to maintain plant diversity on Teesside
- Newcastle University - £7,266. Under the Environment sector
- Beamish – The North of England Open Air Museum - £10,000.

Applications

All applicants should first obtain the Foundation's guidelines from the website – www.esmeefairbairn.org.uk - or by calling 020 7297 4700.

These guidelines set out the specific funding priorities for each sector and include an application form. There is only one set of guidelines which covers all four sectors.

To apply applicants should fill in the short form at the back of the guidelines and write a proposal document about the proposed work – guidance for this is included in the guidelines.

The Foundation can only accept applications by post – you cannot send an application by fax, e-mail or online. There are no deadlines for applications – you can apply at anytime. There are regular trustees' meetings and your application does not need to coincide with any of these. The Foundation does not publish the dates of trustees' meetings.

Before you put together an application for more than £100,000 you should first telephone the Foundation to discuss your proposal.

Exclusions

The Foundation **will not** support:
- Applications from individuals or which benefit one individual
- Applications from organisations which have applied within the previous 12 months
- Work which has already taken place (retrospective grants)
- Work which will not directly benefit people in the UK
- Work which directly replaces statutory funding
- Medical research
- Standard health services and day / residential care
- Animal welfare
- Expeditions and overseas travel
- Endowment funds
- General appeals or circulars.

The Foundation for Sport and the Arts

Correspondent	Grattan Endicott OBE Secretary to the Trustees PO Box 20 Liverpool L13 1HB
Telephone	0151 259 5505
Fax	0151 230 0664
Income	£3 million (01/02)
Grants	£4,844,294 (01/02)
Trustees	Sir Tim Rice, The Lord Brabazon of Tara, Nicholas Allott Esq., The Lord Attenborough CBE, Dame Janet Baker CH DBE, The Rt Hon Sir Christopher Chataway, The Lord Faulkner of Worcester, The Lord Grantchester, Clive Lloyd Esq. CBE, Stephen Roberts Esq., Gary Speakman Esq.
Area	UK
Meets	Two sets of meetings per year

Policy

The Foundation distributes money donated voluntarily by the football pools promoters (Littlewoods and Vernons). Following the introduction of the National Lottery mid-week draw, the funds available to the Foundation have been significantly reduced and the following revised guidelines are in force until further notice.

Grant aid from the Foundation may be made for the support of athletic sport, non-athletic sport or the Arts.

The Trustees will continue to aim very largely to offer grant aid where it will help create or maintain facilities and opportunities for the general community or will assist arts and sports provision that the community can enjoy.

The pursuit of excellence concedes first place to measures to increase participation in, and enjoyment of, sport and the Arts by the whole community, regardless of levels of competence.

The Trustees prefer to support applicants who have never received anything from the Foundation, rather than make further grants to those who have previously received a substantial award. The Trustees are encouraged when they see that applicants are doing what they can to raise money from other sources. In the case of the smallest groups, this may only involve things like coffee mornings, sponsored walks, jumble sales etc.

Schemes in which the Foundation will be the lead funder are preferred, although some grants may be allocated in selected cases as partnership funding where the majority funding is from the National Lottery. In particular, the Foundation may be prepared to take on the principle funding of a discrete segment of such a project where this can be distinguished as a significant, self-contained Foundation exercise (e.g. fitting out a particular gallery within a Lottery-funded building).

The Foundation For Sport and The Arts (Cont...)

Start-up revenue funding could be considered.

Specific guidance is given in the Guidelines for Applicants concerning applications for golf, archery, hang - gliding, parascending, parachuting, gliding, playground equipment, rambling, walking, hiking, shooting, health and fitness, church organs, bands, amateur football, drama / dance students and museums.

Grants

The maximum grant that the Trustees will normally offer has been set at £75,000. The practical maximum in most cases is around £35,000 - £40,000 and lower than this in the majority of cases. The Trustees are also willing to consider making an interest-free loan where this would be appropriate (e.g. to purchase or lease a property, where the borrower has / is likely to have sufficient income to repay the loan).

During 2001 the Foundation awarded 190 grants for the Arts and 867 grants for sports (30 of these were for non-athletic sports).

Applications

Detailed guidelines and a questionnaire to accompany your application are available from the correspondent. The following information should be provided in your application:

- The latest Financial Statements of the enterprise to be assisted
- A description of the purpose for which a grant is sought. Where applicable, this should be backed up with the reports of consultants and professional advisers

- The total cost of the project and the amount desired from the Foundation
- A statement of the way in which it is proposed to fund the project, with information on other money

  which will, or may, be committed alongside that of the Foundation.

A special point should be made to tell the Foundation (where applicable) such information as: -

- How many people will benefit from the project?
- What numbers of people can be accommodated in the auditorium or spectator accommodation?
- The precise nature of the ownership of the club, society, premises, trustees, members' committee or the like
- Information as to the persons who will be involved in the realisation of the plan. Where available and applicable, facts as to suppliers and contractors who will be, or who may be, invited to give effect to the proposals
- A completed questionnaire. This is important – cases are delayed if there is no completed questionnaire
- In the case of a club or organisation, a potted history of its founding, development and future aims.

The Trustees would prefer that your detailed application should be accompanied by a synopsis of the key elements set out on a single page of A4. Videos and books are not encouraged. A photograph or two may be helpful in some cases.

In the case of revenue funding, the following should also be noted:

- It is expected that a Business Plan will be required with closely

The Foundation For Sport and The Arts (Cont...)

- detailed assessments of the revenue expenditure envisaged. Specify staff to be employed and why.
- Trustees will look for lean administration, economic and essential in its structure and practices.
- Trustees should be given details of the other revenue funding anticipated, with information as to the extent to which it has been secured. Bodies that should evidently contribute to the project to be listed and their position statements attached to the plan.
- At some stage, the Foundation's reporting accountants (and, if appropriate, other professional advisers) will be asked to explore the proposals in the Business Plan and inform the Trustees of their findings. If grant aid were offered, adherence to the plan as finally agreed would be a condition of payment of the grant.
- To require prominent, ongoing acknowledgment of any substantial grant aid accepted from the Foundation.

Your completed application will be acknowledged and you will be told the unique reference number under which it is listed in the Foundation's computer system.

Applications are processed on a "conveyor belt" system – the speed at which decisions are made is largely governed by the availability of funds or the speed at which funds are arriving at the Foundation.

As soon as a decision is made that an applicant will not receive a Foundation grant in the current period, the Foundation will write to that applicant.

When an application is approved, the Foundation will send a letter of intent to award a grant and the application will be put in the queue to await funds becoming available.

Letters of offer go out within a few days of fresh funds becoming available, subject to conditions (some general, others particular to that application). After the offer is made, each case is allocated to an external consultant, who often has control over the payment of the grant (in instalments or otherwise). Grantees should consult them before they start to spend the money to find out what proportion of the expenditure they will receive as matters progress.

Exclusions
The following **will not** be considered:
- Requests for top-up grants
- Fees, costs, expenses or other renumeration of non-UK performers and participants
- Visits to the UK from abroad
- Endowment or bursary schemes
- Donations e.g. another trust for onward distribution
- Professional fees and costs of administration (unless explicitly specified in the letter of offer)
- Angling
- Croquet
- Pre-school playgroups
- Maintenance of footpaths which are the responsibility of local authorities
- Requests from commercial applicants for health and fitness
- Musical instruments or uniforms for bands
- Trips abroad
- Film productions
- Motorised sport e.g. motor-racing, flying competitions and competitions with motor propelled craft at sea.

Four Winds Trust

Correspondent	Mrs Jane Simmons Secretary Woodlands Park Lane The Raise Alston Cumbria CA9 3AB
Telephone	01434 381 338
CC No	223794
Income	£51,403 (1997)
Grants	£34,650 (1997)
Trustees	L Insall, J Simmons, E Hambly, K Charity, J Gillett, L Craig- Woods, L Holmes
Area	UK
Meets	Once a year, usually in March

Policy

The Trust did not respond to requests for information, therefore the entry is based on information previously held by FINE.

The Trust's aim is to encourage people to enjoy the countryside and preserve the open country and amenities.

Grants

The Trust awarded 71 grants, totalling £34,650, in 1997. Most grants were for under £1,000. Locally, the following grants were awarded:-
* Newcastle Children's Adventure Group - £750
* Calvert Trust - £750
* Student Community Action Newcastle - £300

Applications

Apply in writing to the correspondent by 31st January. Your letter needs to give the following information:
* Who will benefit
* How many will benefit
* Why the funding is needed
* Amount required
* You also need to send a copy of your latest accounts and any other relevant information.

Exclusions

No grants given to individuals.

Published by FINE (tel: 0191 477 1253)

Joseph Strong Frazer Trust

Correspondent	Joseph Miller & Co Accountants Scottish Provident House 31 Mosley Street Newcastle upon Tyne NE1 4HX
CC No	235311
Income	£516,201 (2001)
Grants	£643,550 (2001)
Trustees	Sir W A Reardon Smith Bt. R M H Read, D A Cook
Area	England and Wales, with special interest in North East England
Meets	March and September

Policy

The Trustees make grants to support charitable institutions and for charitable purposes.

Grants

During 2001 grants were made to support a wide range of charitable activity:

- Children £65,000
- Youth £29,000
- Elderly £17,000
- Hospitals and Homes £51,500
- Deaf and Blind £46,000
- Disabled £31,000
- Mentally Handicapped £11,000
- Medical/Other Research £100,500
- Maritime £36,800
- Armed Forces £6,000
- Care Organisations £69,500
- Schools and Colleges £22,000
- Leisure, animals and wildlife £34,500
- Religious bodies £29,000

Applications

There is no standard application form. Written applications can be made at any time.

Exclusions

Grants are only made to registered charities. No grants are given to individuals.

Maurice Fry Charitable Trust

Correspondent	Mrs F. Cooklyn 13 Quay Walls Berwick upon Tweed TH15 1HB
CC No	327934
Income	£23,932 (2001)
Grants	£40,000 (2002)
Trustees	Lisa Weeks, Angela Fry, Lea Fry
Area	UK and International (with a particular interest in the North East of England)
Meets	November and May

Policy

The Trust is a small family-run grant-making trust which supports registered charities only, however grants may be made via an intermediary charity. The Trust is particularly interested in funding community groups which are based in or around Berwick upon Tweed and surrounding areas.

The Trust are interested in supporting groups working in the following areas of interest:
- Arts / Culture
- Carers
- Children / Young People
- Counselling
- Disadvantaged / Poverty
- Women's Organisations.

The Trust makes both one-off and recurrent grants up to a maximum of three years. Grants will be made for capital items, organisation running costs and project revenue costs.

If applying for a repeat grant the Trust would expect to receive a short progress report.

Grants

Grants range between £250 and £1,000, with most grants awarded in the North East being around £500. During the year to 30/09/2002 the Trust awarded grants to the following organisations:
- The Maltings Trust, Berwick
- The Better Berwick Fund
- Borders Talking Newspaper
- Berwick Youth Project
- Berwick United Reform Church.

Applications

Application is by letter and must include a copy of recent accounts and an annual report.

The application letter must state:
- Purpose of charity and level of need
- Geographical area covered
- Work being undertaken to meet the identified need
- Organisation's track record / level of expertise
- Why grant is required.

Exclusions

The Trust **does not** make grants to individuals.

Paul Getty Jr. General Charitable Trust

Correspondent	Ms Bridget O'Brien Twohig Administrator 1 Park Square West London NW1 4LJ
Telephone	020 7486 1859
Website	www.jpgettytrust.org.uk
CC No	292360
Income	£1,556.773 (2001)
Grants	£1,805.500 (2001)
Trustees	Sir Paul Getty, The Rt. Hon. J Ramsden, C H Gibbs, V E Treves, Lady Getty
Area	UK, with priority going in particular to the inner cities and towns in the northern part of the country.

MeetsQuarterly

Policy

The Trust aims to fund projects to do with poverty and misery in general, and unpopular causes in particular, within the UK. The emphasis is on self-help, building esteem and enabling people to reach their potential.

The Trustees favour small community and local projects which make good use of volunteers. Priority is likely to be given to projects in the less prosperous parts of the country, particularly in the North of England, and to those which cover more than one beneficial area.

Grants are usually in the £5,000 - £10,000 range and those made for salaries or running costs are for a maximum of 3 years. Some small grants of up to £1,000 are also made.

There are four areas which the trust supports, with the bulk of the funding going to social welfare:

Social Welfare
- Mental health in a wide sense, including projects for mentally ill adults, mentally handicapped adults, drug / alcohol / other addictions and related problems, support groups for people under stress (e.g. battered wives, victims of abuse, families in difficulty etc), counselling (especially young people) and mediation.
- Offenders, both in and out of prison, men and women, young offenders, sexual offenders.
- Communities which are clearly disadvantaged trying to improve their lot, particularly projects to do with helping young people in the long-term.
- Homelessness, particularly projects which help prevent people becoming homeless or resettle them.
- Job creation projects or ones aimed at making long-term, constructive use of enforced leisure time, particularly ones set up by unemployed people.
- Ethnic minorities involved in the above areas, including refugees, particularly projects aimed at integration.

Arts
Only the following will be considered - therapeutic use of the arts for the

Paul Getty Jr. General Charitable Trust (Cont..)

long-term benefit of the groups under the Social Welfare programme and projects which enable people in these groups to feel welcome in arts venues and which enable them to make long-term constructive use of their leisure.

Conservation
Conservation in the broadest sense, with emphasis on ensuring that fine buildings, landscapes and collections remain or become available to the general public or scholars. Training in conservation skills. Not general building repair work.

Environment
Mainly gardens, historic landscapes and wilderness.

Both revenue and capital grants are made, but please read the Exclusions category carefully, as it is possible that the particular aspect of your application rather than the general purpose of your organisation may be excluded.

Grants
New grants authorised in 2001 fell into the following categories:
- Community Groups - 23 grants, totalling £353,250
- Mental Health - 13 grants, totalling £129,250
- Family - 14 grants, totalling £176,250
- Youth - 30 grants, totalling £648,650
- Offenders - 7 grants, totalling £141,000
- Drugs / Alcohol - 5 grants, totalling £77,500
- Homeless - 19 grants, totalling £366,600
- Ethnic Minorities - 8 grants, totalling £174,500
- Women - 7 grants, totalling £124,500
- Physically Handicapped - 1 grant, totalling £10,000
- Conservation / Heritage - 24 grants, totalling £69,750
- Environment - 2 grants, totalling £62,000
- Miscellaneous - 10 grants, totalling £17,000.

Applications
Write or ring for a copy of the full guidelines first, or consult the website. After reading them, a letter, no more than 2 pages long, is all that is necessary.

This should give an outline of the project, a detailed costing, the existing sources of finance of the organisation, and what other applications (including those to statutory sources and the National Lottery) have been made. Please also say whether you have applied to or received a grant previously from this trust.

Please do not send videos, tapes or bulky reports - they will not be returned. Annual accounts will be asked for if your application is going to be taken further.

The project will also have to be visited before an application can be considered by the Trustees. This may mean a delay, as it is only possible to visit a small part of the country between each quarterly Trustees' meeting. Three months is the least it can take to award a grant. Some small grants of under £1,000 can be made without a visit, but only for specific purposes.

Applications can be made at any time, and all letters of appeal will be answered, but please remember only 2 pages in the first instance.

Paul Getty Jr. General Charitable Trust (Cont..)

Exclusions

The Trustees **do not** consider applications for the following:

- Individuals
- The elderly
- Children
- Education
- Research
- Animals
- Music or drama (except therapeutically)
- Conferences or seminars
- Medical care (including hospices) or health
- Medical equipment
- Churches or cathedrals
- Holidays or expeditions
- Sports or leisure facilities (including cricket pitches).

Residential projects or large building projects are unlikely to be considered. The Trustees do not support national appeals or grant-giving trusts such as Community Trusts. Headquarters of national organisations and 'umbrella' organisations are unlikely to be considered, as are applications from abroad. Past grant recipients are not encouraged to reapply. The project must be a registered charity or under the auspices of one.

The Goshen Trust (Formerly the Albert Dicken Charitable Trust)

Correspondent	R Oliver Trustee The Goshen Trust PO Box 367 Stockton on Tees TS16 9YR
CC No	274910
Grants	£461,628 (2000/01)
Trustees	A G Dicken, P B Dicken, R Oliver, J R Dicken, A Dicken
Area	Preference for the North East
Meets	Quarterly in March, June, September and December

Policy

The Trustees seek to encourage, support and develop projects which would not ordinarily be able to achieve an effective operation. Such support not only includes seed-funding and parallel matched funding but also ongoing support to enable medium term plans to be formulated and commitments made accordingly. The Trust mainly supports Christian organisations with a preference for the North East of England and a percentage to over-seas work.

Grants

The Trust awarded over 33 grants totalling £461,625 in the year ended 5th April 2001. Grants ranged from under £1,000 to £76,000.

Organisations in the North East which were awarded grants included:
- Emmanuel Fellowship - £73,200

The Goshen Trust (Cont..)

- Christian Institute -   £29,000
- Butterwick Hospice -   £75,000
- Lightfoot Grove Baptist Church
                                £76,200
- Saltburn Mission -   £1,000
- N E Christian Schools -   £20,000
- Christians Against Poverty –
                                 £5,000
- St George's, Normandy -   £2,000
- Turnabout Trust -   £3,120
- Christian Academy -   £5,000

Applications
In writing to correspondent, including a SAE.

Exclusions
None supplied.

Helpful Hint...

Avoid using buzzwords and jargon.

Hospital of God at Greatham

Correspondent	Mr David Granath Director Estate Office Greatham Hartlepool TS25 2HS
Telephone	01429 870 247
Fax	01429 871 469
E-mail	David.Granath@greatham.co.uk
CC No	228571
Income	No information given
Grants	£140,400 (2001)
Trustees	There are eleven Trustees.
Area	The ancient Diocese of Durham (Hartlepool, Stockton, County Durham, Tyne and Wear and Northumberland)
Meets	January, May and October

Policy
The Hospital of God at Greatham was founded and endowed by Bishop Stichill in 1273, primarily as an almshouse charity. Surplus income is distributed in the form of grants for the relief of poverty, sickness or distress either to individuals via social services departments, or to other charitable organisations – preference is given to smaller, low profile charities.

The Hospital of God at Greatham (Cont..)

Grants
Grants awarded range from £50 to £10,000. Occasionally grants are awarded for up to three years.

Applications
Applications by letter preferably including a copy of your latest audited or independently examined accounts and current budget.

Exclusions
The Hospital of God at Greatham **does not** consider applications for:
- Grants towards the capital costs of new buildings
- Purely medical related projects
- Feasibility studies and evaluation costs.

Greggs Trust

Correspondent	Ms Jenni Wagstaff Trust Manager Fernwood House Clayton Road Jesmond Newcastle upon Tyne NE2 1TL
Telephone	0191 212 7626
Fax	0191 281 9536
Email	jenniw@greggs.co.uk
CC No	296590
Income	£758,892 (2001)
Grants	£625,006 (2001)
Trustees	F M E Nicholson, F K Deakin, A Davison, R Hutton, P McKendrick, A Norman, L Spluier
Area	Northumberland, Tyne & Wear, County Durham and Teesside
Meets	Twice each year, in May and November, monthly for grants up to £500

Policy
The main objective of the Trust is the alleviation of poverty and social deprivation, principally within the North East of England, and the Trustees give priority to local, or in certain cases regional, organisations and projects with this objective.

Greggs Trust (Cont..)

Projects in the fields of the arts, the environment, conservation, education and health will be considered so long as they have a social welfare focus and / or are located in areas of deprivation.

There is a strong preference for community-based and locally managed activity, and for estate and neighbourhood-based projects. Recent grants have included support for work with homeless people, older people, young people, children and women, the unemployed and people with disabilities.

Applications from small community-led organisations and self-help groups are more likely to be successful than those from larger and well-staffed organisations, and those which have greater fund-raising capacity. Exceptions may be made where innovative work is being developed by established agencies or where such agencies are providing services to smaller or local groups.

Major grants (i.e. over £1,000) are approved at twice yearly meetings of the Trustees, who are likely to make a few grants of £3,000 - £10,000 per year (in certain cases possibly for more than one year) and a small number of one-off grants of between £1,000 and £3,000.

Small grants of up to £500 (very occasionally up to £1,000) are made to a wide range of local organisations, groups and projects, approved on a monthly basis.

"Hardship" grants to individuals and families are made via recognised agencies twice a month.

The Trustees are committed to equal opportunities and anti-discriminatory practice and wish to encourage applications from disadvantaged groups of all kinds including ethnic minorities, people with disabilities and other minorities, without prejudice as to racial origin, religion, age, gender or sexual orientation.

Grants

The Trust awarded 26 Major grants, totalling £194,475, and 125 Small grants, totalling £62,132. More than 720 grants, totalling £59,128, were also made during the year for families or individuals referred by Social Services, Probation Services and other agencies in the North of England (see entry in FINE's North East Guide to Grants for Individuals for further details).

The Divisional Charity Committees made more than 450 grants, amounting to £227,471.

Major Grants included:
- The Choysez Project, Ashington, Northumberland - £30,000
- Links, Hexham, Northumberland - £10,000
- The Lazarus Foundation, Sunderland - £10,000
- North Tyneside Disability Forum, North Shields - £5,391
- Berwick Family Centre, Berwick, Northumberland - £5,000
- Skills For People, Newcastle upon Tyne - £2,500
- Parents in Need of Support, Hartlepool - £4,000

Small Grants include:
- Abbeyfields First School, Morpeth, Northumberland - £1,000
- Disability Gateshead, Tyne & Wear - £1,000
- Pride on Tyne, Newcastle upon Tyne - £1,000
- Wansbeck CVS, Ashington, Northumberland - £1,000

Greggs Trust (Cont..)

Applications
Applicants should request the policy and priorities leaflets from the correspondent before preparing an application. The Trust does not use an application form for Major or Small grants.

Applications for Major grants can be submitted at any time, but should be sent no later than mid-March or mid-September to be assessed in time for the Trustees' meetings in May and November. The Trust aims to respond to applications for Small grants within approximately 2 months and to acknowledge applications for Major grants in the same period.

Applicants will be informed if their application has not been selected for further consideration. Applications, which have been selected for further consideration, may be visited or contacted for further information.

Exclusions
See Exclusions Leaflet in the policy and priorities guidelines.

The Hadrian Trust

Correspondent	John Parker 36 Rectory Road Gosforth Newcastle upon Tyne NE3 1XP
Telephone	0191 285 9553
CC No	272161
Income	£178,168 (2000/01)
Grants	£178,300 (2000/01)
Trustees	R M Harbottle, B J Gillespie, J B Parker
Area	The boundaries of the old counties of Northumberland and Durham (includes Tyne and Wear and the former county of Cleveland, but only North of the River Tees).
Meets	Quarterly, usually January, March, July and October

Policy
To help social welfare and other charitable organisations within the beneficial area. The main headings under which applications are considered are – Social Welfare, Youth, Women, the Elderly, the Disabled, Ethnic Minorities, the Environment, Education, the Arts and Churches.

Grants are usually one-off, for a special project or part of a project. Core funding is rarely considered. The average grant is £1,000.

The Hadrian Trust (Cont..)

Grants
141 grants, totalling £178,300 were awarded in 2000/01. Grants ranged from £250 to £5,000 (average £1,000) and included the following:

Arts (6 Grants)
- Brinkburn Music - £5,000
- Newcastle Music Group - £500

Churches (8 Grants)
- At Bartholomew's, Kirkwhelpington £1,000
- St Cuthbert's PCC, Bedlington – £2,000

Disabled / Elderly (19 Grants)
- Sharks Wheelchair Basketball Club - £1,000
- North Tyneside Disability Forum - £500
- Hartlepool Access Group – £1,000
- Rainbow Garden Project, Alnmouth - £1,000
- Sunderland MIND - £1,000

Education (6 Grants)
- Longbenton Community College –£1,000
- Newcastle upon Tyne High School Development Trust - £2,000
- The Total Learning Challenge, Newcastle upon Tyne - £1,000

Environment (9 Grants)
- Ryhope Engines Trust, Sunderland - £1,000
- Newcastle Community Green Festival - £500
- Centre for the Children's Book – £5,000

Ethnic Minorities (4 Grants)
- Racial Harassment Support Group, East Heaton - £500
- Hartlepool VDA (for Asylum Seekers Fund) - £500

Social Welfare (36 Grants)
- Rosehill Residents' Association, Wallsend - £1,000
- St Oswald's Hospice, Newcastle - £5,000
- Berwick Family Centre - £500
- Sunderland Kidney Patients' Group - £1,000
- Gateshead Carers Association – £500
- South Benwell Playgroup - £500

Women (8 Grants)
- North Durham Domestic Violence Forum – £1,000
- North Tyneside Women's Aid – £1,000
- The Open Theatre Company, Newcastle - £1,000
- Tyneside Women's Health - £500

Youth (40 Grants)
- Boldon Amateur Boxing Club – £250
- Newburn Leisure Under 14's Football Club - £250
- 1st Barnard Castle Scouts - £1,000
- Longbenton Youth Project - £1,000
- Newcastle City Council for Ouseburn Alcohol-free Bar - £500
- Northumberland Association of clubs for Young People - £2,000

FINE has a full list of all grants awarded.

Applications
If you are unsure whether your project fits within the Trust's general guidelines, you can telephone the correspondent for advice. There is no application form but an information sheet is available on request.

Application is by letter which should set out concise details of the project, the proposed funding and a list of

The Hadrian Trust (Cont..)

other applications being made, with the result if known. A copy of the latest annual report and accounts should be enclosed. Eligible applications will be acknowledged and the acknowledgement will give the date when the application will be considered.

Cheques are sent to successful applicants within 2 weeks of the meeting, but no further correspondence is sent to unsuccessful applicants.

Exclusions
General applications from large, national organisations are **not** considered, nor from smaller bodies working outside the beneficial area. The Trust now allocates a block grant of £16,000 each year to the Greggs Trust to make grants to individuals in need.

W A Handley Charity Trust

Correspondent	Secretary Messrs Ryecroft Glenton 27 Portland Terrace Newcastle upon Tyne NE2 1QP
CC No	230435
Income	Not available
Grants	£338,040 (2001)
Trustees	A Glenton, D Milligan, W Dryden
Area	UK, with a strong preference for Northumberland and Tyneside
Meets	Quarterly in March, June, September and December

Policy
The Trust makes grants in response to applications from within the Northumberland and Tyneside area and from national charities operating within, or where work may be expected to be of benefit to, the Northumberland and Tyneside area. Grants will not usually be made outside these areas.

The main categories of work supported are Youth, Children, Education, Expeditions, Community Welfare, Medical Care, Research and Churches, Church Work.

Grants are usually made for pump-priming, running costs and the alleviation of distress. Crisis funding is also awarded.

W A Handley Charity Trust (Contd..)

Grants

The Trust received over 390 applications in the year ending 5 April 2001 and awarded 168 grants, totalling £338,040.51 were one-off grants and the other 117 were to regular beneficiaries. 99% of grants made were within the Northumberland /Tyneside area, 1% was to benefit the North East generally.

Grants by category were as follows:

- Social Care – 49 grants totalling £81,350
- Health – 31 grants totalling £42.190
- Education – 6 grants totalling £18,400
- Arts, Culture & Recreation – 26 grants totalling £69,350
- Religious Activities – 15 grants totalling £17,200
- Development & Housing – 9 grants totalling £26,550
- Environment & Animal Care – 4 grants totalling £27,000
- Philanthropy, Volunteering & Voluntary Sector Support – 18 grants totalling £17,650
- Science & Technology – 3 grants totalling £30,000
- Civil Society, Law & Advocacy – 6 grants totalling £7,600
- Social Science – 1 grant totalling £750

Applications

In writing to the correspondent, quoting your registered charity number and providing full back up information.

Exclusions

Grants are only given to registered charities. No grants are given to individuals. All appeals received from registered charities to benefit the Northumberland and Tyneside area are considered.

The Hanson Environment Fund

Correspondent	The Royal Society for Nature Conservation The Kiln Waterside Mather Road Newark Nottinghamshire NG24 1WT
Telephone	0870 036 1000
Fax	0870 036 0101
E-mail	grants@rsnc.cix.co.uk
Website	www.hansonenvfund.org
Income	£1,500,030 (2001)
Grants	£2,752,845 (2001)
Trustees	No information given
Area	Within ten miles of Hanson operations – UK wide
Meets	Quarterly for main fund and monthly for community grants scheme

Policy

The Fund makes one-off grants to community groups or not-for-profit organisations who have their own bank account, for work in the following areas:

- Community development
- Environment / Nature conservation
- Recreation
- Community recycling

The Hanson Environment Fund (Cont..)

The Fund offers two levels of support:

Community Grants Scheme – grants between £250 and £4,000 for community amenities, wildlife and habitat conservation and the promotion and instigation of recycling and re-use of waste.

Main Grants Scheme – grants between £4,001 and £25,000 for the introduction of local recycling and re-use of waste and the creation and improvement of parks and public amenities. Projects applying under this scheme must be able to identify matched funding of 10%.

Grants
The Fund awarded grants totalling £2,752,845 during 2001. The following were awarded in the North East:
- Northumberland Wildlife Trust, Wild Waste Community Recycling and Gardening Project, Newcastle – £44,910
- Tees Valley Wildlife Trust, Lustrum Beck Corridor, Stockton-on-Tees - £17,227
- Barrasford Playground Committee, Hexham - £4,000

Applications
Application forms are available from the correspondent, or you can download the form from www.hansonenvfund.org

The Fund requests that you provide as much detail as possible in all sections of the form, as well as enclosing supporting documents where requested, e.g. photographs or plans.

Exclusions
Grants **cannot** be made for the following:
- Research
- Feasibility studies
- Green / environmental business clubs
- Projects leading to commercial benefit
- Student bursaries
- Repair / restoration to places of worship or structures of historic or architectural interest
- Sports halls or other facilities for clubs charging membership fees
- Projects exceeding £100,000 in total (unless the fund is being asked to provide the final amount of funding to make the project happen)
- Purchase of land or buildings
- Purchase of equipment costing more than £5,000
- Core costs of an organisation
- Funding of more than one year
- Retrospective funding

John Haswell Memorial Trust

Correspondent	Victoria Clark Panel Secretary John Haswell House 8/9 Gladstone Terrace Gateshead NE8 4DY
Telephone	0191 478 4103
Fax	0191 477 1260
Minicom	0191 478 4103

E-mail
victoria@gvoc.org.uk

Website
www.gvoc.org.uk

CC No	510764
Income	£6,730 (2001/02)
Grants	£3,714 (2001/02)
Trustees	P Nelson, V Clark, F Lewis, E Ward, J Todd, C Burnett, A Marshall
Area	Gateshead-based organisations or those active in Gateshead only
Meets	Every 2 months

Policy
The John Haswell Memorial Trust is administered through Gateshead Voluntary Organisation Council (GVOC). The sole income is from 1p and 2p coins thrown into fountains in the Metro Centre.

The coins are cleaned and counted by volunteers.

Grants from £25 to £400 are awarded to charitable organisations based and active within Gateshead to help with the costs of new pieces of work or developments. Applications are particularly welcomed from the following:
- From small and newly started groups for furniture, equipment, one-off starting up, project or training costs or for information on model or pilot projects elsewhere which Gateshead groups wish to study.
- From longer established organisations for conferences, training, seminars and initiatives to co-ordinate joint use of resources, or to establish local expertise in areas of use to voluntary organisations

Groups do not have to be registered charities to apply for funds.

Other income comes from the Great North Forest and is only distributed during the summer months to Gateshead / Gateshead-based voluntary groups for travel costs for outings in the Great North Forest area, contact the Panel Secretary for further information.

Grants
15 grants totalling £3,714.10 were made in 2001/02 including:
- Tyneside Foyer - £375.00
- Blue Quarries Residents Association – £65.00
- Cameo Group - £305.00
- Kibblesworth Village Mill Centre – £400.00
- ADHD North East - £325.10
- Route 26 Community Project - £300.00
- Lobley Hill Women's Group - £160.00

John Haswell Memorial Trust (Cont..)

- Emmaville Community, Over 60's Club - £250.00
- Wesley Methodist Church Thursday Toddler - £85.00

Applications

Guidelines and application forms are available from GVOC. The Panel Secretary will contact all applicants to discuss their application in more detail before it is forwarded to the Grants Panel, who meet bimonthly to discuss applications and distribute funds.

Exclusions

Statutory organisations are not eligible to apply.

Grants are **not given** for:

- Individuals
- Salary costs
- Any ongoing running costs of projects
- Partial funding for large, general appeals
- Training course fees outside of the area where expertise will not be shared with other Gateshead groups.

Bill & May Hodgson Charitable Trust

Correspondent	H Straker Trustee Dickinson Dees St Ann's Wharf 112 Quayside Newcastle upon Tyne NE99 1SB
CC No	295313
Income	Not available
Grants	£14,750 (1996/97)
Trustees	R M Wilson, H Straker, Col. G S May
Area	National and International, with some preference for the North East
Meets	Once a year (when sufficient applications have been received)

Policy

The Trust did not respond to requests for information therefore the entry is based on information previously held by FINE.

The Trustees have recently decided to distribute their annual available income amongst the following sectors in the following proportions - children and youth (20%), medical relief (20%), old people and welfare (15%), the Services (10%), environment heritage / arts / culture (10%), overseas aid (10%), local charities (10%) and preservation of wildlife (5%).

Bill & May Hodgson Charitable Trust (Cont..)

Grants
The Trust made 66 grants, totalling £14,750, in the financial year ending 10 October 1997. Grants ranged from £200 to £400.

Applications
The Trust does not have guidelines for applicants and does not use an application form. Applications should be made in writing to the correspondent.

Exclusions
Donations are only made to other registered charitable organisations. No grants are made to individuals.

The Ruth and Lionel Jacobson Charitable Trust

Correspondent	Mrs I R Jacobson MBE Trustee High Wray 35 Montagu Avenue Newcastle upon Tyne NE3 4JH
CC No	326665
Income	£46,658 (2002)
Grants	£57,317 (2002)
Trustees	Mrs I R Jacobson MBE, Mr M D Jacobson
Area	National with a preference to the North East
Meets	Every two months

Policy
Medical, Jewish, children's and disabled people's charities figure prominently among the beneficiaries.

Grants
No information available.

Applications
In writing to the correspondent, quoting your registered charity number and stating why the money is needed. If you enclose an SAE, a reply will be sent (even if unsuccessful).

Exclusions
Grants are only given to registered charities. No grants are given to individuals.

The Joicey Trust

Correspondent	N A Furness FCA Appeals Secretary St Ann's Wharf 112 Quayside Newcastle upon Tyne NE99 1SB
CC No	244679
Income	£483,026 (2000/01)
Grants	£171,900 (2000/01)
Trustees	The Rt. Hon. Lord Joicey, The Rt. Hon. Lady Joicey, Elizabeth Lady Joicey, The Hon. A H Joicey, R H Dickinson CBE
Area	Northumberland and the old metropolitan area of Tyne and Wear
Meets	January and July. Applications must be submitted no later than end November and end May.

Policy

The Trust makes grants to a large number of charities in the North East, many to organisations working in the field of social welfare and youth.

The Trustees support both capital and revenue projects, but tend to favour discrete projects over the support of general running costs.

They do not normally consider recurrent grants, but start-up finance is sometimes available, always providing that the Trustees believe that the project can become viable without the Trust's assistance in a small number of years.

Grants

The Trust made 187 grants during the financial year 2000/01 totalling £171,900. The grants ranged from £100 to £5,000. The majority of grants were under £2,000.

FINE has a full list of all grants made, the following are examples of grants made during 2000/01:

- Newcastle Diocesan Repairs - £5,000
- Northumberland County Scout Council - £5,000
- Northern Counties School for the Deaf - £3,000
- Fulwell Grange Christian School Trust - £2,000
- Northern Pinetree Trust - £1,500
- Red Squirrels in South Scotland - £1,000
- Northumberland Family Camping Group - £850
- Kenton Park Sports Centre- £400
- ME Association; West Northumberland Support Group - £100

Applications

The Trust has no formal application form. Apply in writing, including a brief description of the project. A copy must be attached of the previous year's audited / independently audited accounts and, where possible, a copy of the current year's projected income and expenditure.

Large projects should give an indication as to where the major sources of funding are likely to come from. Unsuccessful applications are not acknowledged unless a S.A.E. is provided with the original application.

The Joicey Trust (Cont..)

Exclusions

National appeals are not supported unless there is specific evidence of activity benefiting the local area.

Applications from the following are not considered:
- Organisations which do not have charitable status
- Personal applications / Individuals
- Organisations that do not have an identifiable project within the beneficial area.

Helpful Hint...

Instead of telling a funder what they want to fund, tell them what you plan to do, how and why – present a clear picture of what will happen, how you plan to proceed and how you'll measure success.

Rose Joicey Fund

Correspondent	Finance Officer Newcastle CVS MEA House Ellison Place Newcastle upon Tyne NE2 8XS
Telephone	0191 232 7445
Fax	0191 230 5640
Income	£4,578 (2001/02)
Grants	£5,270 (2001/02)
Trustees	The Trustees of Newcastle CVS - J Veit Wilson, M Coyle, R Abrahams, V Bagnall, M King, M Shaw, R Wood, T Brown, J Tait, H Cairns, K James
Area	Northumberland, Tyne & Wear and County Durham.
Meets	No information given

Policy

One-off grants ranging from £50 to £200 to groups, individuals or organisations which organise holidays for the needy.

Grants

In the year ending 31 March 2002, the fund awarded 14 grants to organisations, totalling £1,725, and 24 grants to individuals / families, totalling £3,120
Successful organisations included: -
- CEDAR Wood Trust - £150
- Busy Bees - £150
- Pilgrimage Trust - £100
- Mobex - £100
- St Aidens's Parish - £130

Rose Joicey Fund (Cont..)

Applications
By letter to the correspondent, stating the costs, amount sought and other sources approached. Application for individuals by letter via Social Services or similar.

Exclusions
No grants to groups outside the beneficial area or for projects other than holidays for the needy.

The Kelly Charitable Trust

Correspondent	Sir David Kelly CBE Chairman of the Trustees Stanton Fence Morpeth Northumberland NE65 8PP
CC No	1075895
Income	circa £3,000 (2001)
Grants	circa £3,000
Trustees	Lady Kelly, Georgina Charlton, Chloe Allport, Daisy Kelly, Francesca Kelly
Area	Mainly Northumberland, Tyne & Wear, County Durham
Meets	Infrequently, but as required.

Policy
This small family trust was established in 1999. It has no written guidelines and the Trustees consider each application on its own merit, but particularly award grants supporting voluntary work where the participants are known to the Trustees.

One-off grants to registered charities and voluntary organisations are given for capital items, organisation running costs, project revenue costs, building work and to individuals.

Monitoring and evaluation of grants is not usually required as the Trustees only donate to organisations which provide evidence of and/or the

The Kelly Charitable Trust (Cont..)

Trustees have confidence in effective management procedures.

Both successful and unsuccessful applicants should wait 3
years before re-applying to the Trust.

Grants
Grants from £25 to £1,000.

Applications
Applications should be in writing addressed to the correspondent, providing a simple explanation of the organisation and how the grant will be used.

Exclusions
None given.

The Sir James Knott Trust

Correspondent	Vivien R Stapley Trust Secretary 16 –18 Hood Street Newcastle upon Tyne NE1 6JQ
Telephone	0191 230 4016
CC No	1001363
Income	£1,200,000 (01/02)
Grants	£1,108,510 (01/02)
Trustees	Viscount Ridley, The Hon O F W James, M R Cornwall-Jones, C A F Baker-Cresswell
Area	Northumberland, Tyne & Wear and County Durham (including Hartlepool)
Meets	Three times a year, normally February, June and October

Policy
The Trustees have wide discretion on the distribution of funds.

In recent years, grants have been given in support of Universities, general education, training, medical care and research, historic buildings and the environment, music and the arts, as well as the welfare of the young, the older people, seamen's and service charities, disabled people and those who are disadvantaged.

Grants
A total of 665 applications were processed in 2001/02, with 304 grants made, ranging from £250 to

The Sir James Knott Trust (Cont..)

£100,000. The average size of grant was around £4,000.

Summary By Area:
- Northumberland - 71 grants totalling £256,700
- Tyne & Wear – 121 grants totalling £378,550
- County Durham – 59 grants totalling £283,700
- North East in general – 40 grants totalling £158,500

Summary By Category:
- Community Welfare – 108 grants totalling £389,850
- Youth / Children – 68 grants totalling £192,950
- Education / Expeditions – 12 grants totalling £136,860
- Heritage / Museums – 21 grants totalling £101,650
- Handicapped – 29 grants totalling £78,750
- Service Charities – 22 grants totalling £58,950
- Conservation / Horticulture – 9 grants totalling £42,000
- Elderly – 8 grants totalling £33,000
- Medical – 9 grants totalling £27,000
- Maritime Charities – 9 grants totalling £22,500
- Arts – 7 grants totalling £19,000
- Housing / Homeless – 2 grants totalling £6,000

FINE has a full list of all grants made in 2001/2002. Here are some examples:
- Chester le Street and District CVS, County Durham - £2,000
- Durham Association of Clubs for Young People - £10,000
- Elswick Girls Project, Newcastle - £2,000
- Friends of Southlands School, North Shields - £500
- Greenhead Village Hall Committee, Northumberland - £4,000
- Hebburn Neighbourhood Advice Centre (via South Tyneside CVS) - £5,000
- Invalids at Home, North East - £2,000
- King's Own Scottish Borderers, Berwick – £2,000
- Lazarus Foundation, Sunderland - £3,000
- Monster Theatre Productions, Wallsend (via North Tyneside VODA) - £2,000
- Newton Aycliffe Over 60s Club, County Durham - £3,000
- Ord Parish Hall, Berwick - £2,000
- Pegswood Miners' Welfare, Northumberland - £3,000
- Sea Cadets, Ashington - £1,000
- Together We Can Manage, Newcastle (via Newburn Community Association) - £1,000
- Unity Organisation, Sunderland - £2,000
- Victim Support, Tynedale - £3,000
- Who Cares? North East (via Families in Care) - £5,000
- YMCA, North Eastern Division - £8,000

Applications
The Trust does not publish guidelines for applicants. Brief written applications should be sent to the correspondent, stating who you are, how you are organised / managed, what your aims are, how much you need, what for and when, how much you are asking the Sir James Knott Trust for and how you plan to raise the rest (if any).

If you do not have your own registered charity number, you need to provide the registered charity number of an organisation which is willing to administer the funds on your behalf. You also need to send a copy of your most recent Trustee report and accounts.

The Sir James Knott Trust (Cont..)

NOTE – there could be a 6-month wait to hear whether you have been successful.

Exclusions
Grants are only made to registered charities in the North East of England (see area of benefit).

No grants are made to individuals. A few annual donations are made to national charities, but only if they benefit the North East.

Helpful Hint...

The contact person named in the letter should know everything about the application.

The Allen Lane Foundation

Correspondent	Heather Swailes Executive Secretary 90 The Mount York YO24 1AR
Telephone	01904 613223
Fax	01904 613133

E-mail
enquiries@allenlane.demon.co.uk

Website
www.allenlane.demon.co.uk

CC No	248031
Income	£467,516 (2001/02)
Grants	£518,281 (2001/02)
Trustees	C Morpurgo, C Teale, Z Teale, J Walsh, J Walker, G Dehn
Area	UK, with priority for work outside London
Meets	Three times a year, usually in February, June and October

Policy
The size of grants (which are modest) are particularly appropriate for start-up costs of smaller projects, grants for equipment, training for staff and volunteers, small evaluations and one-off projects etc. Grants can be made for project costs and core costs.

As the grants are small it is rare for an application for salaries to be eligible, but a contribution to other core costs may be suitable.

The Allen Lane Foundation (Cont..)

The Trustees make grants to organisations whose work they believe to be unpopular, with priority groups being refugees and asylum-seekers, black and ethnic minority communities, gay men, lesbians and bi-sexual people, those experiencing mental health problems, older people, offenders and ex-offenders, and travellers, amongst others.

The broad areas of work which are priorities for the Trustees include:
- The provision of advice, information and advocacy
- Community development
- Neighbourhood mediation, conflict resolution and alternatives to violence
- Research and education aimed at changing public attitudes or policy
- Social welfare aimed at making a long term difference and empowering users

The Foundation targets about 80% of its grant-making towards national or regional organisations of a modest size and around 20% on local projects. One-off grants for projects generally range from £250 to £10,000 – grants to local projects are usually between £750 and £3,000. Revenue grants of £1,000 to £5,000 a year may be made for up to three consecutive years.

Grants
During 2001/2002 the Trustees made 114 new grants totalling £504,279. 44 of these grants were under £3,000.

Grants in the North East in 2001/2002 were as follows:
- First Stop Darlington, towards core costs of information service - £3,000 over 2 years
- Studio 64, for musical activity and training with local refugees - £2,000

- Conflict Response in Schools Programme, for the cost of training facilitators for conflict work in schools - £3,000
- Independent Advocacy, for an independent evaluation - £2,000
- Hartlepool Asian Association, for start up costs of a community centre - £750
- The Comfrey Project, to pilot a scheme to promote well-being among asylum seekers – £3,000
- Bliss Mediation Service, core costs - £3,000 over 2 years

Applications
Grants are made to organisations for charitable work. "Guidance for Applicants" which explains how to apply can be found at The Foundation's website, www.allenlane.demon.co.uk The site also provides detailed guidance for applicants, lists all grants made and closing dates for each meeting of the Trustees.

Applicants should plan well ahead to allow sufficient time for applications to be assessed – as the Trustees only meet three times a year, it could be as long as four months before you hear whether you have been successful.

The Foundation will not normally consider an application within a year of an earlier refusal.

Exclusions
The Foundation **does not** generally make grants for the following:
- Academic research
- Addiction, alcohol or drug abuse
- Animal welfare or animal rights
- Arts or cultural or language projects or festivals
- Children and young people
- Disability issues
- Holidays or holiday play schemes, sports or recreation
- Housing

The Alan Lane Foundation (Cont...)

- Individuals
- Large, general appeals from charities which enjoy widespread public support
- Medical care, hospices or medical research
- Museums or galleries
- Overseas travel
- Private and/or mainstream education
- Promotion of sectarian religion
- Publications
- Purchase costs of property, building or refurbishment
- Restoration or conservation of historic buildings or sites
- Vehicle purchase
- Work which the Trustees believe is rightly the responsibility of the state
- Work outside the United Kingdom
- Work which will already have take place before a grant is agreed.

Lankelly Foundation

Correspondent	Peter Kilgarriff Director 2 The Court High Street Harwell Didcot Oxfordshire OX11 0EY
Telephone	01235 820 044
Website	www.lankelly-foundation.org.uk
CC No	256987
Income	£4,650,346 (00/01)
Grants	£5,091,471 (00/01)
Trustees	S Turner, L Fraser-Mackenzie, Lady Merlyn-Rees, G Campbell, S Raybould, N A Tatman
Area	UK, except Greater London area and Northern Ireland
Meets	Quarterly

Policy
The Trust supports small registered charities which meet local needs. The Trustees look for user involvement as well as proper use and support of volunteers.

The minimum grant is £5,000 and grants are always made for specific purposes but they may cover capital or revenue needs. Revenue support to a maximum of five years will be considered although three-year support is more the norm.

Lankelly Foundation (Cont...)

Until 2004 the Trustees' priorities are:

Elderly People
Projects which demonstrate the promotion of improved quality of life, independent living and user involvement will be considered.

Families and Children
Applications are invited from projects which support people and young children (under 13 years) who are marginalised because of poverty, unemployment or crime, including domestic and sexual abuse.

Homelessness
Grants will focus on preventative work with young people and support to older homeless people who need long term support in resettlement and in particular ex-offenders, refugees, elderly homeless people and those with multiple problems.

Mental Health
Support will be given to projects which promote independence and reintegration into society, combat isolation whether geographical or cultural, support those who are particularly vulnerable such as the elderly people, homeless people and those in secure accommodation.

Neighbourhood Work
Grants will be targeted at small voluntary agencies with a strong user involvement, particularly in areas of high levels of poverty and disadvantage. Support will be given to those who are working to create a positive environment.

Penal Affairs
Consideration will be given to projects that contribute to the rehabilitation of those in prison and those leaving prison and to the support of their families and friends.

Physical and Learning Disabilities
The Trust particularly wishes to receive applications for projects which promote independent living and social inclusion, through advocacy, training, sheltered and supported work opportunities.

Young People
Supports work with young people aged 14-25 years, particularly those who are vulnerable, living in deprived neighbourhoods, at risk of school exclusion or offending, including youngsters leaving local authority care.

Grants
The Foundation made 6 grants to organisations in the North East of England, totalling £213,000, including:
- Bliss Mediation Services, Blyth Northumberland - £29,000
- Kids Kabin, Newcastle - £30,000
- Scotswood Area Strategy, Newcastle – £84,000
- Calvert Trust, Kielder - £15,000
- Fawdon Community Association, Newcastle - £15,000
- St Margaret's Community Project, Scotswood, Newcastle - £40,000

Applications
The Foundation does not use an application form. The leaflet "Information for Applicants" sets out in detail the application process and what to include in your letter of application.

Exclusions
In general terms the Trustees **do not** contribute to large, widely circulated appeals.

More particularly grants are not given in support of:
- Adaptations to improve access to Arts and heritage
- Advancement of religion

Lankelly Foundation (Cont..)

- Animal welfare
- Buildings
- Conferences or seminars
- Endowment funds
- Festivals or theatre productions
- Hospices
- Individuals
- Individual youth clubs
- Large capital projects
- Medical research
- Other grant making bodies
- Publications, films or videos
- Schools for people with special needs
- Sport
- Travel, expeditions or holidays
- Vehicles

William Leech Charity

Correspondent	Mrs K M Smith Trust Secretary Saville Chambers 5 North Street Newcastle upon Tyne NE1 8DF
CC No	265491
Income	£653,293 (00/01)
Grants	£1,536,361 (00/01)
Trustees	P H Baylis, R E Leech, C J Davies, A Gifford, N Sherlock, D A Stabler, R D Leech, B Wallace
Area	The counties of Northumberland, Tyne & Wear and Durham
Meets	Six times a year

Policy

Grants and fixed term interest free loans are made to registered charities at the discretion of the Trustees, who place great emphasis on those who are voluntarily helping others.

Applications from charities where at least two thirds of the charitable work is done by volunteers are especially preferred, although the Trustees recognise that this work sometimes needs to be carried out by qualified, and therefore paid, staff.

The number of applications received from larger charities with paid workers or from professional fundraisers has increased as has the number of applications received from organisations traditionally supported by Local Authorities - these are all

William Leech Charity (Cont.)

considered, but are lower priority for the Trustees.

Charities with an active Christian involvement, or working in deprived areas for the benefit of local people (especially those which encourage people to help themselves) or doing practical new work / putting new ideas into action are preferred, as are independent boys' and girls' clubs, YMCA, YWCA, Scouts, Guides etc.

Pump-priming grants are usually in the range of £50 - £100. A large number of grants are given in the £250 – £1,000 range, with larger grants of up to £10,000 for new projects (sometimes support is given for up to 3 years, to allow a project to get off the ground). Fixed term interest free loans of up to £10,000 may also be made, usually for emergency church repairs.

Approximately one third of the annual income is allocated to the University of Newcastle upon Tyne. Occasionally large grants of £50,000 to £150,000 are given to major local appeals.

Lady Leech Third World Fund
This fund of around £40,000 a year has been set up to distribute to third world projects which have, if possible, a strong personal connection with the beneficial area (the counties of Northumberland, Tyne & Wear and Durham). Grants will be up to £5,000 and are only given to registered charities (NOT individuals).

Grants
The Trust awarded 174 grants, totalling £1,536,361, in the year ending 28 February 2001.

FINE has a full list of all grants made – the following are some examples:
* Action for Blind People - £1,000
* Balliol Youth Centre, Longbenton - £2,000
* Berwick Mind - £500
* Childline, Yorkshire & North East - £500
* Diocese of Newcastle - £250
* Eastgate Village Hall, Durham - £1,000
* Faramir Trust - £250
* Gateway Club, Hexham - £250
* Lady Hoare Trust - £1,000
* MENCAP - £250
* NCTC - £2,500
* Northumberland County Scout Council - £2,000
* Riverside Netball Club - £100
* South Tyneside Stroke Club - £250
* The Outdoor Trust Northumberland - £500
* Wheels Project, South Shields - £1,000
* YMCA Newcastle - £5,000

Applications
Written applications should be no longer than one A4 page, and should include the following information as a minimum:-
* Charity name and registration number (or number of charity willing to accept donation on your behalf)
* Name of applicant and address
* Details of the project, its aims, progress, funds raised so far and how much is still required and for what purpose
* Number of paid staff
* Annual salary costs and total administration overheads
* Number of unpaid volunteers

Applications should be sent to the Correspondent.

William Leech Charity (Cont.)

The Trust does not acknowledge receipt of applications, but does inform all applicants as to the outcome of their application. It can take up to 3 months to process an application.

Exclusions
The following will generally **not** receive grants:
- Community centres and similar (except very occasionally those in remote country areas)
- Running expenses for youth clubs
- Running expenses for churches, including normal repairs, unless engaged in social work or using the building largely for "outside" purposes
- Sport
- The Arts
- Individuals
- Holidays, travel and outings
- Minibuses
- Schools
- Housing Associations
- Organisations which have been supported in the last 12 months, except where agreed in advance

Lloyds TSB Foundation for England and Wales

Correspondent	Peter Ellis Manager – North East PO Box 779 Newcastle upon Tyne NE99 1YJ
Telephone	0191 261 8433
Fax	0191 244 6235
Minicom	020 7204 5276

E-mail
peter.ellis@lloydstsb.co.uk

Website
www.lloydstsbfoundations.org.uk

CC No	327114
Income	£24.9 million (2001 – nationally)
Grants	£23.5 million (2001 – nationally)
Trustees	J Foster, Rev. R Benson, V Burton, J A Penny, Prof. M Stewart, L Quinn, H Phillips, Dr P Lane, C Webb, K Singh
Area	England and Wales (there are separate Foundations for Scotland, Northern Ireland and the Channel Islands)
Meets	The Board of Trustees meet quarterly to approve donations

Lloyds TSB Foundation for England and Wales (Cont..)

Policy

The overall policy of the Trustees is to support under-funded charities which enable people, especially disadvantaged or disabled people, to play a fuller role in the community. The Trustees encourage applications for core funding or for funding towards specific items, but prefer not to make contributions towards large appeals, e.g. for building costs.

The Foundation has two main objectives to which it allocates funds:

Social and Community Needs
A wide range of activities are supported, including Advice Services, Community Relations, Community Facilities and Services, Disabled People, Promotion of Health and Cultural Enrichment.

Education and Training
The objective is to enhance learning opportunities for disabled and disadvantaged people of all ages e.g. literacy skills, pre-school education, promotion of life skills and independent living skills.

The Trustees regularly review changing social needs and identify specific areas they wish to focus on within their overall objectives. The areas of special interest outlined in the guidelines for applicants in 2000 will apply for a minimum of three years and are:

Family Support – particularly work which aims to equip people with relationship, parenting and caring skills, and to provide the support needed to be effective parents and carers. There is a specific focus on enabling men to play a more active role in parenting and caring, developing and improving relationships between generations, helping young people (especially those in or leaving care) to develop relevant life-skills and supporting families coping with challenging behaviour.

Challenging Disadvantage and Discrimination – particularly work which aims to raise awareness of these issues and to promote the involvement of all people within society. There is a specific focus on helping disadvantaged people to participate in decision-making processes which affect their lives, promoting understanding and encouraging solutions which address disadvantage, discrimination or stigma and challenging disadvantage, discrimination and stigma within the field of mental health.

Promoting Effectiveness in the Voluntary Sector – particularly work which aims to improve management skills and to promote collaborative working and sharing of good practice. There is a specific focus on supporting the development of regional voluntary sector networks, encouraging communication and collaboration, supporting the training of Trustees, managements, staff and volunteers and encouraging organisations to review and assess the effectiveness of their work.

Areas of special interest for 2003 onwards.
The areas of special interest will remain the same for 2003. The Foundation will review the specific focus within these headings during 2002, and these may be amended for 2003.

The areas of special interest for 2004 onwards will be announced in the

Lloyds TSB Foundation for England and Wales (Cont..)

Guidelines published by the Foundation during 2003.

The Foundation for England and Wales is the largest of the four Foundations, receiving 72% of the total income, the majority of which is allocated to regional budgets.

Donations to local projects which fall within the areas of special interest can be up to £10,000, sometimes over two or more years.

Donations to local projects which do not fall within the areas of special interest are up to £5,000 and are one-off. Applicants are strongly advised to seek advice from the Foundation before applying for sums in excess of these ranges, or for funding over 2 or more years.

Up to 5% of the Foundation's income has been set aside to match fundraising efforts by members of staff within Lloyds TSB Group of England and Wales – up to £500 per person per year for charities which fall within the Foundation's guidelines.

Grants

In 2001 the North East Regional Office made 242 grants totalling £1,354,836. The average size of grant was £5,598. Grants awarded included the following:

- Greenhead Village Hall - £2,570 towards general running costs and equipment
- St Paul's Community Project - £6,000 towards the salary of a Project Worker
- Cleveland Arts - £5,000 towards the Bridge Project
- CAB – Castle Morpeth - £5,000 towards core funding

- Air Training Corps – 1338 Seaham – £2,250 towards the purchase of one go-kart
- Multiple Sclerosis Society – South Tyneside - £2,000 towards the installation of a ramp into the Society's caravan at Haggerston Castle
- Parish of All Saints and Salutation, Blackwell - £2,651 towards the costs of tables and stacking chairs for the Church Hall
- Rape and Sexual Abuse Counselling Centre (Darlington and County Durham) - £3,000 towards salary of a part-time employee
- Alzheimer's Society, Darlington - £10,000 for the cost of a salary for a branch manager
- North East Post Adoption Service - £4,500 towards salary of a post adoption worker
- CVS, Blyth Valley - £10,000 for training for groups
- Sedgefield Out of School Fun Club - £2,025 towards employment of a special needs worker
- Chester-le-Street Sea Cadet Corps - £1,500 towards new equipment
- Lukes Lane Community Association, Hebburn - £1,850 towards residential weekend for young people

Applications

Guidelines and application forms are available from the Foundation's office and can be returned at any time.

Guidelines are also available in audio format. All applications are reviewed on a continual basis and the Board of Trustees meets quarterly to approve donations.

Decision making processes can therefore take up to three months, but all applicants are informed of the outcome of their applications. Over 50% of all applications to the

Lloyds TSB Foundation for England and Wales (Cont..)

Foundation were successful in 2001. Successful applicants are advised to leave at least two years before applying for further support.

Unsuccessful applicants should leave at least one year before reapplying.

Exclusions

The main areas of concern normally considered to be outside the Foundation's guidelines are:

- Organisations which are not registered charities
- Activities which are primarily the responsibility of central of local government or some other responsible body
- Activities which collect funds for subsequent redistribution to other charities or to individuals
- Animal welfare
- Corporate affiliation or membership of a charity
- Endowment funds
- Environment – conservation and protection of flora and fauna, geographic and scenic
- Expeditions or travel overseas
- Fabric appeals for places of worship
- Fundraising events or activities
- Hospitals and Medical Centres (except for projects which are clearly additional to statutory responsibilities)
- Individuals, including students
- Loans or business finance
- Overseas appeals
- Promotion of religion
- Schools, universities or colleges (except for projects specifically to benefit disabled people or which are clearly additional to statutory responsibilities)
- Sponsorship or marketing appeals

The Mahila Fund

Correspondent	Zulfiqar Ahmed C/o The Pukaar Foundation West Bowling Centre Clipstone Street Bradford BD5 8EA
Telephone	01274 735551
Fax	01274 305689
Email	info@ged-uk.org
Income	No information available
Grants	No information available
Area	London and North East England
Meets	Once a year

Policy

The Trust did not respond to requests for information the entry therefore is based upon FINE research.

The Mahila Fund is part of the Pukaar Foundation. The fund will give grants to individual women or women's organisations that have a turnover of less than £500,000 per annum.
The Mahila Fund supports activities such as:

- Individual women to enable them to make a difference to their communities
- Training and education
- Development of organisations and social enterprise
- Outreach work

The Mahila Fund (Cont..)

- Education around the use of complementary medicines.

Successful applicants are expected to
- Use the funds as outlined in their application
- Return unspent funds
- Provide a report on how the grant was used
- Provide accounts, receipts and bank statement if requested

Grants
Grants are made up to a maximum of £500.

Applications
For application details and pack, send a A4 SAE to the correspondent.

Exclusions
No information given.

R W Mann Trustees Limited

Correspondent	J. L. Hamilton OBE Secretary PO Box 119 Gosforth Newcastle upon Tyne NE3 4WF
Telephone	0191 284 2158
Fax	0191 285 8617
E-mail	John.Hamilton@onyx.octagon.co.uk
CC No	259006
Income	£144,918 (2000/01)
Grants	£141,074 (2000/01)
Trustees	J A Hamilton, G Javens, M Heath
Area	Tyneside area with a preference for North Tyneside
Meets	Monthly

Policy
The Trust's objectives are:
- The relief of the poor, aged or infirm
- The advancement of education and public religion, and
- The promotion of social welfare of a charitable nature

Grants made vary between regular annual donations, small one-off donations and grants for capital projects. The average size of grant awarded is £1,000.

Most of the beneficiaries in recent years have been youth groups (both

R W Mann Trustees Limited (Cont..)

uniformed and non-uniformed), children, people with disabilities, older people, schools, colleges, councils for voluntary service and other advice agencies.

Grants

In the year ending 31st March 2001, the Trust awarded 123 grants, totalling £141,074. FINE has a full list of grants awarded, of which the following are examples:

- 16th Whitley Bay Boy Scout Group - £2,000
- Anchor Trust – Holly Court - £100
- Bede's World - £2,000
- Cullercoats Community Association - £400
- East End Baby Equipment Loan Scheme - £750
- Meadow Well Credit Union Ltd - £500
- Monkseaton Community High School - £200
- Newcastle Jellicoe Sea Cadets - £1,500
- North Sea Volunteer Lifeguards - £500
- Northumbria Youth Action - £4,000
- Shieldfield & Battlehill Community Project - £1,000
- The "Not Forgotten" Association for Disabled - £100
- Theatre of Incurable Players - £3,000
- Tyneside Kidney Patients Association - £200
- Walker Central Football Club – £2,000
- Whitley Bay Y.M.C.A - £5,000

Applications

Written applications to the correspondent at any time. Applicants should send an S.A.E with their application.

Exclusions

The Trustees are unable to make grants to individuals except in the form of particular educational scholarships through the University of Newcastle.

Helpful Hint...

Don't think of a letter to a trust as a 'begging letter' – the money in a trust has to be spent on charitable work so you are giving them the opportunity to spend it.

Leslie and Lilian Manning Trust

Correspondent	K. L Andersen
Trustee
Watson Burton
20 Collingwood
Street
Newcastle upon Tyne
NE99 1YQ
CC No	219846
Income	Not available
Grants	£25,000 - £30,000
each year
Trustees	N Sherlock, P Jones,
D Jones, K L
Andersen
Area	Mainly in the North
East of England
Meets	Twice a year (May &
November)

Policy
The Trust gives regular support to a number of health and welfare charities and makes one-off discretionary awards to other organisations in the North East.

Grants
No information available.

Applications
In writing to the correspondent, for consideration at the meeting of the Trustees.

Exclusions
Buildings, education and individuals are not supported.

Sir Stephen Middleton Charity Trust

Correspondent	Mrs S E Bolam
Trustee
Estate Office
Belsay
NE20 0DY
CC No	276351
Income	No information given
Grants	No information given
Trustees	M Mortimer, S E
Bolam
Area	Northumberland and
Newcastle upon Tyne
only
Meets	Normally every three
months

Policy
The Trust will only consider applications in writing from charities supporting local and public interest.

Grants
No information was available.

Applications
In writing to the correspondent.

Exclusions
None supplied.

Millfield House Foundation

Correspondent   Terence Finley
Administrator
19 The Crescent
Benton Lodge
Newcastle upon Tyne
NE7 7ST

Telephone   0191 266 9429

Fax   0191 266 9429

E-mail
finley@lineone.net

Website
www.newnet.org.uk/mhf

CC No   271180

Income   £280,501 (2000/01)

Grants   £158,905 (2000/01)

Trustees   J McClelland, S McClelland, W G McClelland, R Chubb, G Hepburn

Area   Tyne & Wear and North East England

Meets   May and November

Policy

The Trustees wish to encourage applications which propose radical improvement of social conditions in the North East of England, particularly Tyne & Wear.

Applications are invited from organisations which are located in, or have an impact on, the communities of Tyne & Wear. The Trustees support proposals which elucidate and tackle the fundamental causes of deprivation rather than simply alleviating it.

Applications should have any of the following aims:

- To seek to influence the policy of national, regional or local government and other public bodies and to inform and educate opinion on social, economic and political issues.
- To enable the voluntary sector as a whole, individual voluntary and community organisations and those who benefit from their services to contribute to policy and debate from first hand experience of social need and current conditions, by campaigning for the improvement of such policy and public provision.
- To develop activities which may have been proven in other parts of the UK but have not been developed in Tyne and Wear or which, through being tested in Tyne and Wear, could provide models for practice and development elsewhere, particularly activities which empower people and communities to meet their own needs and exploit their own resources.

The financial resources available to the Foundation are a tiny fraction of the total available for charitable activity in Tyne and Wear. The Trustees therefore wish to concentrate their resources on objects which most other funding bodies cannot or will not support.

As a charity, the Foundation must confine its grants to purposes accepted in law as charitable. However, official guidance makes it clear that charities may include a variety of political and campaigning activities to further their purposes.

Millfield House Foundation (Cont..)

(Political Activities and Campaigning by Charities CC9, published by The Charity Commission in 1995, was revised in 1999 mainly by the addition of a section on the involvement of charities in demonstrations and direct action. It can be viewed and printed from www.charity-commission.gov.uk

The Foundation wishes to promote equal opportunities through its grant-making. It will do its best to ensure that applications are dealt with fairly and that no one is denied access to information or funding on grounds of race, colour, ethnicity or national origin, religious affiliation, gender, sexual orientation, age or disability. If appropriate, the Foundation will offer help with the completion of an application.

The Foundation welcomes applications from stand-alone projects, from organisations which sponsor or manage projects, or from two or more projects applying jointly.

In certain cases, and strictly subject to compliance with Section 6 of the Charity Commission's guidance on Political Activities and Campaigning (CC9), the Foundation may be willing to support proposals which involve non-violent direct action.

The Trustees are willing to take some risks in funding projects which strongly reflect the stated priorities. The Administrator is available to discuss and give guidance on the submission of innovative proposals.

The Millfield House Foundation aims to provide, alone or in partnership with other funders, significant and medium-term support to a small number of carefully selected projects or organisations.

The Foundation is unlikely to have more than about 6-12 grants in payment at the same time and can therefore approve only a small number of new grants in any one year. In some cases, the Trustees may consider a small grant to support work needed in preparation for a major grant. Grants are unlikely to exceed a total of £20,000 for one, two or three years.

Grants
The Foundation made 18 grants, totalling £158,905.30 in the year ending 5th April 2001, including:
- Children North East, Fathers Plus - £10,000
- Church Action on Poverty North East - £4,000
- Crime Concern, Neighbourhood Safety Project, Blyth - £10,000
- The Low Pay Unit, study on poverty and transport – £6,355
- Newcastle Healthy City Project, Ban Waste Group - £12,000
- North East Family Centre Network - £22,500
- North of England Refugee Service, Refugee Advisory Committee on Tyneside (ReACT) - £3,950
- Northumbria Sight Service, Empowerment Project - £12,500
- The Total Learning Challenge - £15,000

A list of examples of recently or currently funded projects may be seen on the Foundation's website, or may be requested from the Administrator.

Applications
Applications should be in writing and include the following:
- Full contact details, including e-mail address if available.

Millfield House Foundation (Cont..)

- A detailed description of the project, its aims and intended outcomes.
- A budget for the project for which a grant is sought, giving a breakdown of total expenditure and of any other sources of income. Where an application is submitted by a sponsoring body, a budget for the organisation as a whole should also be provided for the year(s) for which the application is made.
- A copy of the most recent annual report and audited accounts for the project and/or the sponsoring body. If more than six months have passed since the latest audit, a signed statement of income and expenditure for the period should also be provided.
- The constitution of the responsible body or a brief summary
- Details of the organisation's policy and procedures for Equal Opportunities
- If appropriate, plans for dissemination of the results of the project
- Details of internal and/or external arrangements for monitoring and evaluation of the project for which a grant is sought, including indicators for measuring its longer-term impact
- If funding is sought towards the costs of a salaried post, a job description
- The names of two independent referees. (References will not be taken up in every case).

Exclusions
Generally, the Foundation **does not** make grants:
- Not related to the needs of people in Tyne and Wear

- To large, well-established national charities, or in response to general appeals
- For work in the arts, medicine or conservation
- For buildings, or for purely academic research
- To make up deficits already incurred, to replace withdrawn, expired or reducing statutory funding, or to provide what should properly be the responsibility of statutory agencies
- To meet the needs of individuals
- For travel / adventure projects, or educational bursaries
- To projects likely to qualify for statutory, European Union or National Lottery funding, or likely to appeal to most local or national charitable trusts or similar sources. The Foundation will only consider a contribution in such cases if there is a particular part of the project which other sources would be unlikely to fund
- For the delivery of a service, however great the need, unless it contributes to any of the aims listed in the "Policy" section, in which the Trustees are particularly interested.

Northern Electric Employees Charity Association (NEECA)

Correspondent	Jill Jones Personnel Co-ordinator NEDL Kepier Farm Durham City DH1 1LB
Telephone	0191 333 5922
Fax	0191 333 5932

E-mail
jilljones@northern-electric.co.uk

Website
www.allenlane.demon.co.uk

CC No	1026188
Income	No information available
Grants	No information available
Trustees	Executive committee
Area	Northern Electric's geographical area only
Meets	Approximately every ten weeks

Policy
Applicants must be registered charities.

Grants
No information available.

Applications
In writing to the correspondent.

Exclusions
No grants for building maintenance or in response to applications from outside Northern Electric's geographical area.

Helpful Hint...

Write in short sentences, using shorter rather than longer words. Keep it short and simple but make sure you get your points across clearly and logically.

The Northern Rock Foundation

Correspondent	Fiona Ellis Director Woodbine Road Methodist Church Woodbine Road Gosforth Newcastle upon Tyne NE3 1DD
Telephone	0191 284 8412
Fax	0191 284 8413

E-mail
generaloffice@nr-foundation.org.uk

Website
www.nr-foundation.org.uk

CC No	1063906
Income	Est. £13 million (2003)
Grants	£12.500,000 in 2002 (approx.)
Trustees	L P Finn, P R M Harbottle, The Lord Howick of Glendale, Lady Russell, J P Wainwright, D Baker, D Faulkner, J Shipley, F Nicholson
Area	The North East of England (Northumberland, Tyne & Wear, County Durham and Teesside) and Cumbria.
Meets	At least 5 times a year

Policy

The Northern Rock Foundation was formally launched in January 1998 with an initial donation of £1million from Northern Rock plc, which has covenanted to pay 5% of its pre tax profits to the Foundation each year. The Foundation is fully independent of Northern Rock plc and its policies are determined by its own Board of Trustees.

The primary objective of the Northern Rock Foundation is to help improve the conditions of those disadvantaged in society. Applications from self-help organisations and those that are managed by or can show close involvement of the intended beneficiaries are preferred.

Grants may be made for limited capital, core or project funding and for varying periods of time.

The Foundation's primary purpose is to help disadvantaged people, in particular those disadvantaged due to;
- age – for example, the young and the old
- disability
- displacement – for example, refugees, asylum seekers, survivors of domestic violence
- the collapse of industry or other kinds of employment
- geography – where people live may affect their ability to get basic services, to work together for mutual benefit or to enjoy a healthy and fulfilled life
- prejudice and discrimination, for example against gay men and lesbians or black and minority.

The Northern Rock Foundation (Cont..)

Detailed guidelines are available, which organisations should read before applying. Projects which will be supported must fall into one of the following grant programmes.

Prevention of local and regional social decline – actions which stop social problems from developing or worsening. In particular work around,
- Persistent crime
- Prejudice and discrimination
- High rates of teenage pregnancy
- The difficulties of providing good parenting
- Substance misuse and abuse
- Environmental decay
- Youth disaffection
- Inadequate facilities for local groups to meet including community centres and village halls

Smaller groups which may lack the experience and skills to gather, manage projects and articulate their needs to others who should help them, will be provided with additional financial help to buy in extra expertise if needed.

Regeneration – local initiatives which improve the economic prospects of an area or a community of interest. For example, the creation of more social businesses or money to help development trusts, alternative ways of providing local jobs, facilities and services or training programmes and schemes that help people in an area acquire skills or confidence to re-enter the workplace. Projects in both urban and rural areas that clearly help towards the economic development of the place will be considered. This may include capital grants for buildings or equipment where there is clear economic benefit.

Basics – day to day services.
This programme is aimed at supporting organisations that "add high quality services and assistance to people over and above what statutory authorities provide"
The following organisations are the priorities within this programme;
- In the field of disability, projects designed to benefit people with mental health issues or learning disabilities
- Projects that help people to retain independence, remain in their own homes and benefit from the work of advocacy services
- Carer's organisations
- Refugees and other support for survivors of domestic violence
- Money, debt and welfare advice, establishing credit unions and other schemes to help, people with limited means to manage their money

Exploration and experiment – researching, trying out, thinking, finding new ideas or ways to address social problems. Examples include, action research into new ways of treating persistent offenders, practical research into the causes of disadvantage or social problems.

A Better, Stronger Voluntary Sector – making the sector more capable of helping itself and others, articulating its needs and fighting its corner. The programme is aimed at countywide or regionally based umbrella groups which provide the training, advice and support that enables smaller organisations to develop and thrive. They want to help them provide a better service. The Foundation are particularly interested in organisations that promote quality both in their work and as an example to others.

The Northern Rock Foundation (Cont..)

Aspiration – assistance to cultural environmental, heritage and sporting charities which raise the profile of the area and make it a better place in which to live and enjoy life.

This will support organisations that provide enjoyable and stimulating activities of the highest quality to the widest population. Examples include
- Arts projects
- Museums
- Environmental or outdoor amenities
- Heritage sites
- Charitable sports clubs

To be eligible to apply organisations should have a constitution. You do not have to be a registered charity but the purpose for which you are applying must be charitable according to law and you must be allowed by your constitution to take on the task you propose. You are more likely to be successful if your organisation is led by or has strong representation of the people you are trying to help.

Grants
Grants are given for core support, project and capital grants. Under certain circumstances the Foundation may make loans or invest in organisations in other ways.

Grants awarded are announced after each Trustee meeting. You can write to the Foundation, enclosing an A4 SAE, to obtain a full list of all grants made. The information will also be available on the Foundation's website.

In 2001 44% of grants were for £10,000 or less. In total the Foundation made 405 grants, the average size of which was £27,300 Small organisations with an annual expenditure of less than £25,000 are unlikely to receive a grant of more than £15,000.

The Foundation operates a fast track process whereby organisations which apply for £15,000 or less can, if necessary, have their application processed more quickly.

The following are examples of grants made under the previous grants programme in the North East of England:
- Skills for People - £63,671 over 2 years to involve people with learning disabilities living in Newcastle in the planning and delivery of their local services.
- Fenham Association of Residents – a one off grant of £8,000 towards office equipment for a new community centre.
- Kids Under Cover – a one-off grant of £5,000 to provide a outside play area for the children of Hebburn.
- Age Concern – North Tyneside - £60,953 over 3 years towards activities designed to encourage healthy lifestyles and improve social networks
- Broomhill and District Allotment Association - a one-off grant of £10,000 towards the building of new headquarters to benefit older gardeners in an ex-mining community in Northumberland
- Artscope – a one-off grant of £5,000 towards an art based project focusing on safety and fire prevention at the new South Shields Fire Station.
- Tyneside Cinema - a one-off grant of £63,100 towards the redevelopment of the Newcastle art cinema.

The Northern Rock Foundation (Cont..)

- Chatt – a one-off grant of £2,500 to employ a consultant to train board members in the financial responsibilities of Trustees, and to devise a fundraising strategy for a new organisation based in Durham.

Applications

Guidelines and application forms for the different grant-making programmes are available from the Foundation's office and can be returned at any time.

It is possible, by special arrangement, for groups to apply on tape or video - please discuss this with Foundation staff.

Completed application forms should be returned, along with a brief supporting statement (no more than two A4 pages) describing, the timetable for the project, how the project meets the Foundation's objectives, your own organisation, its aims and the procedures which qualify it to take on this project, the amount requested from the Foundation, the overall project budget and information about applications to other funding sources, and how you will evaluate the project.

You should also attach a copy of your current year's budget and most recent management accounts and a copy of your most recent Annual Report and audited or independently verified accounts.

Your application will be acknowledged and you will be told which staff member is dealing with it and roughly how long it could take (normally 3 months). You may or may not be visited or questioned further about the application and the Foundation may ask others about your project.

Exclusions

Grants **will not** be awarded to:

- Organisations which do not have purposes recognised as charitable in law
- Charities which appear to have excessive unrestricted or free reserves (up to 12 months' expenditure is normally acceptable) or are in serious deficit
- National charities which do not have a regional office or other representation in the North East
- Grant-making bodies seeking to distribute grants on behalf of the Foundation
- Open ended funding agreements
- General appeals, sponsorship and marketing appeals
- Corporate applications for founder membership of a charity
- Retrospective grants
- Replacement of statutory funding
- Activities primarily the responsibility of central or local government or health authorities
- Individuals and organisation that distribute funds to individuals
- Animal welfare
- Mainstream educational activity, schools and educational establishments
- Medical research, hospitals, hospices and medical centres
- Medical treatments and therapies including art therapy
- Fabric appeals for places of worship
- Promotion of religion
- Expeditions or overseas travel
- Minibuses, other vehicles and transport schemes except where they are a small and integral part of a larger scheme
- Holidays and outings
- Playgrounds and play equipment

The Northern Rock Foundation (Cont..)

- Private clubs or those with such restricted membership as to make then not charitable
- Capital bids purely towards compliance with the Disability Discrimination Act
- Amateur arts organisations
- Musical instruments
- Sports kit and equipment

Helpful Hint...

Ask someone outside your organisation to read your application.

Northumberland Foundation for Young People

Correspondent	Jim Anderson c/o County Hall Morpeth Northumberland NE61 2EF
CC No	1049462
Telephone	01670 533 924
Income	£7,099 (1996/97)
Grants	£12,185 (1996/97)
Trustees	S Cram, K Morris, M Davey, I Swithenbank, J Axelby, S Bramley, G Pritchard
Area	Northumberland only
Meets	Quarterly

Policy
The Trust did not respond to requests for information the entry therefore is based on information previously held by FINE

The objects of the Foundation are to preserve and protect good health (both mental and physical), to relieve poverty and sickness, to advance education and to assist in the provision of facilities in the interests of social welfare, recreation or other leisure time occupation for people in need to improve their conditions of life in Northumberland.

The Foundation gives grants for charitable purposes of up to £2,000 to groups dealing with young people

Northumberland Foundation for Young People (Cont..)

(usually under 25 years) and also assists individuals within Northumberland.

Grants

8 groups were awarded a total of £9,820 in 1996/97.

- Calvert Trust, Kielder - £1,020 for respite care for 3 disabled youngsters
- Children North East, Tynedale - £1,100 to purchase a reconditioned engine for RAFT playbus
- Riverbank Department, Ashington - £1,000 towards a skiing trip for disabled youngsters
- NYMCA, Ashington - £1,500 to purchase gym equipment for use by both disabled and able-bodied youngsters
- Grove Special School, Tweedmouth - £1,200 to fund 5 pupils with special needs to attend Calvert Trust facility at Kielder
- Blyth Valley Disabled Forum - £1,000 towards mobile integrated summer activity programme
- Northern Outlook - £2,000 towards costs of outward-bound activities for visually impaired children and their families
- Hackwood Park School, Hexham - £1,000 towards cost of trip to France for children with learning difficulties

Applications

Application forms are available from the correspondent. The Trustees consider applications at quarterly meetings.

Exclusions

Applications, which **will not** benefit young residents of Northumberland.

Northumberland Rugby Union Charitable Trust

Correspondent	D F Hamilton Woodvale Wylam Northumberland NE41 8EP
CC No	1001976
Income	£56,779 (April 1997)
Grants	£24,534 (1996/97)
Trustees	D F Hamilton, A S Appleby, S W Bainbridge, W G Miller
Area	Northumberland, Newcastle and North Tyneside
Meets	No information supplied

Policy

The Trust did not provide up to date information. The entry is based upon information held on the Charity Commission database and additional FINE research.

The Trust provides, grants for up to three years to organisations, including schools to provide training and playing facilities for rugby union to children and young people up to the age of 21.

Grants

Grants can be one-off or for capital, core costs, running costs and salaries. Grants seem to range between £50 and £5,000.

Applications

In writing to the correspondent.

Exclusions

Projects for people over the age of 21.

Northumberland Village Homes Trust

Correspondent	Derek McCoy Probate and Trust Manager Savage Solicitors Bellwood Buildings 36 Mosley Street Newcastle upon Tyne NE1 1DG
Telephone	0191 221 2111
CC No	225429
Income	No information given
Grants	£49,000 (2000/01)
Trustees	D Welch, B Porter, R Baron Gisborough, E P Savage, K Hunt, D McCoy
Area	Priority for the North East of England
Meets	Once a year, usually in November

Policy
The Trust was established in 1880 to relieve poverty, distress and sickness among children and young people under the age of 18 and to promote their education and training. Grants are made to organisations working with children and young people.

Grants
In the year ending 31st March 2001 the Trust made 10 annual grants, totalling £40,000 and 29 discretionary awards, totalling £9,000.
Annual grants ranged from £2,000 to £14,000 and included:
- Barnardo's North East - £5,000
- Children North East - £14,000
- St Cuthbert's Care - £3,000
- Turning Point, Whitley Bay - £2,000

Discretionary awards ranged from £200 to £500 and included:
- Boys Brigade 8th Hartlepool Battalion - £200
- Consett Churches Detached Youth Project - £300
- Re-solv - £500
- Walker Park Play Centre - £300
- West Farm Neighbourhood Community Association - £300
FINE has a full list of grants awarded.

Applications
Apply in writing to the correspondent. Applications should include the following information:
- Registered charity number and objects of charity
- Amount required and why
- Any other sources of funding

Exclusions
Grants are only made to registered charities. No grants are given for medical purposes.

Northumbria Historic Churches Trust

Correspondent	Canon J E Ruscoe Secretary The Vicarage South Hylton Sunderland SR4 0QB
Telephone	0191 534 2325
Fax	0191 2704141
CC No	511314
Income	No information given
Grants	No information given
Trustees	The Rev N Banks, G Bell, C Downs, T R Fenwick, G E R Heslop MBE, J B Kendall, Dr R A Lomas, Mrs B D Napier, Lady Sarah Nicholson, J H N Porter, Canon J E Ruscoe, Canon C P Unwin, R R V Nicholson
Area	The Diocese of Newcastle and Durham
Meets	Quarterly

Policy
The Trust did not respond to requests for information therefore the entry is based on information previously held by FINE.

The Trust is involved in raising money in order to make grants to churches and chapels built more than 100 years ago. Grants are only given for conservation work (e.g. re-pointing of stonework, renewals of roofing, renewals of lightning conductors, restoration and protection of important stained glass, treatment of dry rot, survey work).

Grants
No information given.

Applications
Only apply to the trust if your church is at least 100 years old and you have already applied to the main grant-aiding bodies (English Heritage, the Heritage Lottery Fund, the Historic Churches Preservation Trust etc). The Trust has an application form, available from the correspondent, which you should complete in black ink. Where appropriate, support your application with photographs.

Exclusions
No grants for improvements, extensions, adaptations, heating, lighting, bells, organs, stone cleaning, work on ancillary buildings or church halls or for costs arising out of a failure to insure a church.

Sir John Priestman Charity Trust

Correspondent	Mr P W Taylor Trustee Messrs Mckenzie Bell 19 John Street Sunderland SR1 1JG
CC No	209397
Telephone	0191 567 4857
Income	No information available
Grants	£251,602 (1996)
Trustees	J R Kayll, R J Heslop, J R Heslop, R W Farr, P W Taylor, T R P S Norton
Area	County Borough of Sunderland and Durham County
Meets	Quarterly (January, April, July and October)

Policy
The Trust did not respond to requests for information therefore the entry is based on information previously held by FINE.

The Trust makes a large number of donations to charitable organisations to maintain churches / church buildings and to clergy / church officials and their families in County Durham and Sunderland.

Grants
In the year ending 31 December 1996, the trust made 166 grants, totalling £251,602. These included 36 grants to churches, totalling £85,900, and 92 grants to charitable organisations, totalling £104,805. Grants ranged from £100 to £5,216, with the majority under £2,000.

Applications
In writing to the correspondent.

Exclusions
No grants made outside County Durham and Sunderland.

Helpful Hint...

Explain how you hope to fund your project after the current grant period.

The Ragdoll Foundation

Correspondent	Lydia Thomas Director Russell House Ely Street Stratford upon Avon Warwickshire CV37 6LW
Telephone	01789 773 059
Fax	01789 773 059

Email
info@ragdollfoundation.org.uk

Website
www.ragdollfoundation.org.uk

CC No	1078998
Income	circa £100,000
Grants	£154,762 (2000/2001)
Trustees	Anne Wood, Mark Hollingsworth, Katherine Wood, Ann Burdus
Area	United Kingdom with a particular interest in the North East of England and the Midlands
Meets	Four times a year

Policy

The Foundation was established in 2000. The focus of the Foundation is to make grants to projects, activities or events which promote the development of young people through the arts.

The Trustees give priority to applications which concentrate on young children aged 0-8 years old, although appropriate projects for older children will also be considered.

Projects need to be imaginative, creative and innovative. In particular the Trustees are keen to support strategic initiatives intended to deal with causes of problems and projects which may influence thinking and good practice elsewhere.

The aims of the Trust are to award grants to projects which;
• Promote the development of children through the arts.
• Promote the use of the arts as a healing or development tool for the benefit of children.
• Encourage innovation and innovative thinking by the promotion of best practice in the use of the arts in the development of children.
• Encourage and ensure effective evaluation of projects to promote best practice.

The Trust will also make grants to individual children up to the age of 18 years where the award will add to the development of their potential, progress and well-being.

Grants

Grants range from £300 to £25,000 plus. Both one-off grants and recurrent grants up to a maximum of three years for project revenue costs are awarded.

Three grants were made to organisations in the North East of England in the year ending March 2002:
• The Forge, Durham - £16,070
• Redcar Women's Aid - £300
• Spennymoor School, Durham - £4,972

Applications

Printed guidelines are available from the Trust's office. Applications in writing are accepted from registered charities and voluntary organisations which should include the following information;

The Ragdoll Foundation (Cont..)

- The purpose for which the grant is sought and how the grant will make a difference.
- Full budget details (including how the budget has been determined) and the total grant required
- Information about other funds secured or committed.
- The aims and purposes of the organisation including legal status and registered charity number
- A copy of the latest annual report and audited accounts
- Evidence of monitoring and evaluation procedures.

The Trustees state that the initial work on a grant application may involve discussion and consultation, further development or modification and where possible an on-site visit or meeting(s). They prefer to progress matters steadily to give time for full and thorough consideration of each proposal.
The Trust welcomes exploratory telephone calls from potential applicants.

Exclusions
Applications for the following are **not** considered;
- Animal welfare charities
- Any large capital, endowment or widely distributed appeal
- Charities which are in serious deficit
- Emergency relief work
- General fundraising or marketing appeals
- Holidays
- Loans or business finance
- Open ended funding arrangements
- Promotion of religion
- Replacement of statutory funding
- Retrospective funding
- Work that has already started or will have been completed while the application is being considered.

The Rank Foundation

Correspondent	Mrs Sheila Gent Assistant Grants Administrator PO Box 2862 Whitnash Leamington Spa CV31 2YH
Telephone	01926 744550
Fax	01926 744550
E-mail	rank@dircon.co.uk
Website	www.rankfoundation.com
CC No	276976
Income	£8,200,000 (2000)
Grants	£7,400,000 (2000)
Trustees	F A R Packard, M D Abrahams CBE DL, J A Cave, A E Cowen, M E T Davies, MRS L G Fox JP DL, J R Newton, D R Peppiatt, V A L Powell FCA, Dr. M J Scurr MRCP, MRCGP, The Lord Shuttleworth JP, D R W Silk CBE MA, Earl St Aldwyn
Area	UK
Meets	Quarterly

Policy
The Foundation provides one-off grants of £200 upwards to registered charities. The Directors tend towards appeals where there are relatively

Rank Foundation (Cont..)

small, attainable targets and evidence of local support is of great importance. The main objectives are:

Promotion of the Christian Religion – by means of the exhibition of religious films or any other lawful means.

Promotion of Education There are 2 strands to the programme.
• Education – The Directors take a broad view when interpreting this objective and include work with young people which is designed to involve them in decisions which affect their future and to cultivate in them attitudes which will make them useful members of society.
• Youth -The Foundation believes that young people should be encouraged to develop to the full extent of their potential and wish to support organisations and projects, which have this as their focus.

Any other objectives or purposes which are exclusively charitable according to the laws of England in force. – the directors tend towards appeals which have relatively small, attainable targets and they place great importance on clear evidence of local support.

The Directors are active in identifying initiatives to support in the first two programmes and the funds available for major grants are currently committed.

Grants
The Rank Foundation made grants totalling £7,400,000 in 2000. The following are examples of those made in the North East:
• Northumbria Youth Action - £500
• Alnwick District Playhouse - £2,000

• Great North Air Ambulance - £2,000
• Mobex North East - £78,200
• Middlesbrough Activity Resource Centre - £31,300
• Newcastle YMCA - £30,587

Applications
There are no formal guidelines. The following information is required:
• Charity name and registration number
• Brief details about the project and the amount to be raised
• Details of the amount raised so far towards the target
• Copy of the last audited accounts and annual report.

The Directors meet quarterly and applications will be notified when their appeal is to be considered.

All unsolicited applications are assessed on their individual merits.

Exclusions
In general, grants **will not** be made for:
• Agriculture and farming
• Cathedrals or churches (except where community facilities form an integral part of the appeal)
• Individuals or applications from organisations on behalf of individuals
• Overseas

The Foundation is unlikely to fund:
• Salaries
• General running costs
• Major capital projects

Ravenscroft Foundation

Correspondent	J E Ravenscroft Chairman 763 Durham Road Low Fell Gateshead Tyne and Wear NE9 6PD
Telephone	0191 487 7614
CC No	282359
Income	£5,365.43 (2001/02)
Grants	£5,210 (2001/02)
Trustees	J E Ravenscroft, S E Ravenscroft, K Ravenscroft
Area	Gateshead
Meets	As often as necessary

Policy
This is a small, private trust which distributes money on a one-off basis to a variety of charities and individuals.

Grants
The Foundation awarded 38 grants, totalling £5,210 in the year ending 31st January 2002.
Grants to groups included:
- Parkhead Primary School - £100
- Parents Enquiry North East - £100
- High Town Methodist Church - £50
- Hill Top School PTA - £100
- Whitley Bay Sea Cadets - £100
- Tonbridge YFC - £100

Applications
Apply in writing to the correspondent.

Exclusions
None supplied.

Ropner Centenary Trust

Correspondent	Mr P C Scott Trustee 6 Stratton Street LONDON W1X 5FD
CC No	269109
Telephone	0207 4080123
Income	£50,000 1996/97)
Grants	£36,000 (1996/97)
Trustees	Sir J B W Ropner, J V Ropner, M J Kingshott, D A Winduss, P C Scott
Area	The North East of England
Meets	Twice a year, July and December

Policy
The Trust did not respond to requests for information therefore the entry is based on information previously held by FINE

Grants are only made to registered charities, with a preference for shipping-related and other charities in the North East of England.

Grants
In 1997/98, the Trust awarded 134 grants, totalling £36,000. Grants ranged from £200 to £2,000.

Applications
In writing to the correspondent. Please send only one sheet, which shows your charity registration number and briefly describes the project for which you are seeking funding.

Ropner Centenary Trust (Cont..)

Exclusions
Grants are only made to registered charities.

Helpful Hint...

Say thank you and keep in touch – if a funder knows what you are up to, they're more likely to fund you again.

The Ropner Trust

Correspondent	John Wilson Clerk to the Trustees 22 High Street Stockton-on-Tees TS18 1LS
Telephone	01642 675 555
Fax	01642 678 924
CC No	1062362
Income	£45,800 (2001/02)
Grants	£52,900 (2001/02)
Trustees	M Taylor, R Cook, J Wilson, J Still, H Smith, R Darley, W Pickersgill
Area	Stockton-on-Tees only
Meets	Quarterly

Policy
In addition to promoting the education (including social and physical training) of persons under the age of 25 years who are in need of financial assistance and who are, or whose parents are, resident in Stockton-on-Tees, the Trustees also make grants to charities, sports clubs and other institutions or organisations to use solely for the benefit of Stockton-on-Tees and its residents.

Grants
There were 79 grants awarded, totalling £52,953 during 2001/2002.
- 1 grant over £5,000
- 4 grants £2,000 - £4,999
- 9 grants £1,000 - £1,999
- 65 grants under £1,000

The Ropner Trust (Cont..)

Applications
Guidelines and application forms are available from the correspondent.

Exclusions
No grants for the relief of rates, taxes or other public funds. Grants are only made to benefit Stockton-on-Tees and its residents.

Helpful Hint...

Provide hard evidence (facts and figures) in support of your application.

Rothley Trust

Correspondent	Mrs Diane M Lennon Secretary MEA House Ellison Place Newcastle upon Tyne NE1 8XS
Telephone	0191 232 7783
Fax	0191 232 7783
E-mail	diane_lennon@rothley-rust.fsnet.co.uk
CC No	219849
Income	£141,530 (2000/01)
Grants	£122,869 (2000/01)
Trustees	Dr H A Armstrong, R P Gordon, R Barkes, R R V Nicholson, A Galbraith, C J Pumphrey, J Brown, C Bucknall, G Salvin
Area	Northumberland, Tyne and Wear, County Durham and the former county of Cleveland. For the foreseeable future no applications from North Yorkshire will be considered.
Meets	Quarterly, usually in February, May, August and November

Policy
The main grant-making activities of the Trust are directed exclusively towards smaller charities in the North East of England (including Third World appeals arising from the region).

Rothley Trust (Cont..)

The Trustees prefer to support specific project costs, such as equipment or repairs to premises.

Generally, the Trust supports work in the following categories:
*   Children / Youth
*   Community
*   Education
*   Disabled people
*   Medical
*   Religion (see exclusions)
*   Third world

The grants awarded at the quarterly meetings are usually for small capital costs, with an average grant being £200.

Grants
The Trust awarded 198 grants, totalling £122,869 in the year ending 5th April 2001; this included a donation of £40,021 towards the cost of administering the MEA Trust. 12 grants were made towards school fees and 2 grants were for overseas expeditions.

Examples of grants awarded to organisations during 2000/01 included:
*   Air Training Corps 226 Squadron, Stockton on Tees - £225
*   Alnwick Community Association - £200
*   British Agencies for Adoption and Fostering - £750
*   Prudhoe Street Mission - £1,000
*   Relate, Northumberland and Tyneside – £1,500
*   Citizens Advice Bureau, Newcastle - £3,300
*   Headland Amateur Boxing Club - £150
*   Multi Agency Crime Prevention Initiative - £200
*   St Cuthbert's Hall, Shotley Bridge - £250

*   Victim Support Scheme, Middlesbrough - £150
*   Wear Body Positive, Sunderland - £200

FINE has a full list of all grants awarded.

Applications
Apply in writing to the correspondent, enclosing a stamped addressed envelope. Applications from the beneficial area will be acknowledged.

Exclusions
Grants are only made to registered charities.

No grants are made for:
*   Further education
*   Repair of buildings used primarily for worship (grants given to church organisations are for the community work of local charities)
*   Organisations for older people ex-services / the arts / wildlife
*   Sponsorships
*   Feasibility studies
*   Medical Research

Christopher Rowbotham Charitable Trust

Correspondent	Mrs C A Jackson Trustee – Chairman 18 Northumberland Square North Shields Tyne and Wear NE30 1PX
CC No	261991
Income	£43,000 (2001)
Grants	£38,000 (2001)
Trustees	Mrs C A Jackson, Mrs E J Wilkinson, R M Jackson Esq.
Area	National, with more interest shown to North East and North West England
Meets	Once a year in September

Policy
To support selected national charities including those with branches in the North East and North West of England, but with priority being given to small local charities with low overheads.

Grants
The following grants were made in the North East in 2001:
- Alzheimer's Disease Society, North East - £500
- ADAPT - £250
- Army-Navy-Air force, North East - £250
- British Red Cross (for North East) - £500
- Breast Cancer Campaign (for North East) - £250
- Calvert Trust, Kielder - £1,000
- Crossroads (for North East) - £500
- Cancer Bridge - £250
- CARE Ponteland - £500
- Different Strokes North East - £500
- Disability North - £500
- Donor Families North East - £250
- Fairbridge in Tyne and Wear - £1,250
- Friends of the Laing Art Gallery - £500
- Geordie Jaunts - £300
- Grange Welfare Association - £500
- Hexham Youth Initiative - £500
- North of Tyne Search and Rescue Team – £500
- Northern Pinetree Trust - £250
- North of England Cadet Forces Trust - £2,000
- Northumbria Daybreak - £750
- National Trust (for North East) - £500
- Opening Learning Centre - £250
- Project 2720M - £250
- Raleigh International (for North East) - £750
- Rainbow Trust - £500
- RABI (for North East) - £750
- Riding for the Disabled (for North East) - £500
- RUKBA (for North East) – £750
- R.V.I. Breast Cancer Appeal - £500
- Rural Minds (for North East) - £250
- Salvation Army (for North East) - £500
- Samaritans (for North East) – £750
- Sea Cadets (for North East) - £650
- St Oswald's Hospice - £1,500
- Stamfordham First School - £750
- Tyne Sound News - £250

Applications
The Trust does not publish guidelines for applicants nor does it use an application form. Groups should not

Christopher Rowbotham Charitable Trust (Cont..)

contact the Trust by telephone. Written applications can be sent at any time but are not acknowledged.

Exclusions
Grants are made to registered charities only.

Grants are not given:
* For salary costs
* To individuals, including students
* In response to general appeals from large organisations
* Overseas work
* For capital projects.

The Royal Victoria Trust for the Blind

Correspondent	Mr A E Veitch MBE C/O Lismore 17 Benwell Grange Avenue Newcastle upon Tyne NE15 6RP
Telephone	0191 273 3934
CC No	528072
Income	£31,040 (2001/02)
Grants	£17,447 (2001/02)
Trustees	MR A E Veitch MBE, Miss M S Coulson, Mrs S Taylor, Mrs Y Robinson, Mrs A Ruddick, MR D Walker, Mr W Stafford, Rev. Canon P Strange
Area	Northumberland, Cumbria, Tyne & Wear, County Durham, Teesside and North Yorkshire
Meets	January, March, May, July, September and November

Policy
The Trust awards recurrent grants to organisations working with or for visually impaired people. Grants are available for capital items, organisation running costs and project revenue costs, to a maximum of £10,000.

Grants
During the financial period 2001/02 a grant of £892 was awarded to

The Royal Victoria Trust for the Blind (Cont..)

Newcastle Society for Blind People, towards the cost of a tactile arts course.

Applications
Applications should be made on the Trust's application form and supported by a local society for visually impaired people or social services. Applications for equipment should be accompanied by an appropriate estimate of cost. Successful applicants may re-apply for funding, continuing funding or for a different project at any time.

Unsuccessful applicants should not re-apply for the same project / purpose.

Exclusions
The Trust **cannot** fund the following:
- Holidays (unless there are exceptional circumstances) or educational breaks for children
- Repayment of debts / arrears.

Rural Youth Trust

Correspondent	Tanner Shields OBE Secretary 52 The Hamlet Leek Wootton Warwick Warwickshire CV35 7QW
CC No	1003944
Telephone	01926 511202
Income	£29,228 (2000)
Grants	£24,534 (1997)
Trustees	Sir J Cotterell Bt DL, Lord Plumb DL MEP, A Evans CBE, P Jackson CBE, J Sayers, T Shields OBE, A Woodward
Area	Rural areas of England and Wales
Meets	Twice a year, usually December and July

Policy
No updated information was received from the Trust; the entry is based upon information previously held by FINE and that which appears on the Charity Commission database.

The Trust aims to support effective voluntary youth work of the kind provided by the Young Farmers' Movement with, and on behalf of, young people from 11 to 26 in the rural areas of England and Wales.

The Trustees give priority to applications for projects which motivate young people, provide training in leadership, improve young people's understanding of their role in

Rural Youth Trust (Cont..)

society and encourage young people to take part in environmental activities or to participate as full and caring members of their rural communities. Grants are generally limited to £2,500 per organisation and can be used towards the purchase of training expertise and materials or to support conferences, training courses and projects within the criteria of the Trust.

Grants
9 grants, totalling £15,300, were made in 1997. Two of these were in the North East:
•   East Durham Community Development Initiative - £250
•   Teesside Community Resources - £500.

Applications
The Trust has very detailed notes on the criteria for applicants, which you should get hold of before applying.

Exclusions
The following are **unlikely** to be supported:
•   administration and administrative staffing of projects
•   formal education projects under the auspices of Local Education Authorities
•   international travel
•   projects where statutory or other funders have withdrawn
•   equipment (unless necessary to complete an approved project).

St. Hilda's Trust

Correspondent	Mr P Davies Secretary Church House St. John's Terrace North Shields NE29 6HS
Telephone	0191 270 4100
Fax	0191 270 4141
CC No	500962
Income	Not available
Grants	£54,700 (1997)
Trustees	The Bishop of Newcastle, The Archdeacon of Northumberland, R P Gordon, Dr M J Wilkinson, E Wright, Mrs R Nicholson
Area	The Diocese of Newcastle (includes North Tyneside and Northumberland)
Meets	Quarterly in January, April, July and October

Policy
The Trust did not respond to requests for information therefore the entry is based on information previously held by FINE.

The objects of the Trust are to "further such legally charitable purposes in connection with the Church of England in the Diocese of Newcastle as the managing Trustees of the Trust may think proper. In particular, the relief (either generally or individually) of

St. Hilda's Trust (Cont..)

persons who are in conditions of need, hardship and distress".

The current main areas of concern are young people generally and, in particular, today's equivalent of the original young people of St Hilda's School and those whose needs are not met by state social welfare provision. Organisations do not need to be registered charities, but must have charitable purposes.

Grants
The Trust awarded 27 grants, totalling £54,700, during 1997. A number of grants were for more than one year. Grants ranged from £200 to £5,000

Applications
Guidelines and an application form are available from the correspondent.

Exclusions
No grants are given for work outside the Diocese of Newcastle or for Operation Raleigh / Project Trust type ventures.

Storrow Scott Charitable Will Trust

Correspondent	G W Meikle Esq Trustee Dickinson Dees St. Ann's Wharf 112 Quayside Newcastle upon Tyne NE99 1SB
CC No	328391
Income	No information given
Grants	£34,110 (1996)
Trustees	G W Meikle, J S North Lewis
Area	Preference given to the North East of England.
Meets	Once a year, in July

Policy
The Trust did not respond to requests for information therefore the entry is based on information previously held by FINE.
The Trust makes donations to a wide range of groups, both local and national, including medical research, children, youth groups, crime-related projects, communities and education.

Grants
The Trust made 12 grants, totalling £10,150, in the year ending 5 April 1996. Grants ranged from £150 to £2,750.

Applications
In writing to the correspondent.

Exclusions
No grants are given for minibuses (or similar vehicles) or to students wanting to make overseas trips.

Sedgefield Charities

Correspondent	R Smeeton Clerk to the Trustees 13 North Park Road Sedgefield County Durham TS21 2AP
Telephone	01740 620 009
CC No	see policy
Income	£24,650 (2001)
Grants	£23,065 (2001)
Trustees	The Rev M Q King, S Margerison, Dr C J Hearman, P T Terry, T J Sheenan, G K Wells, E Mason, G G Wright, S Traynor, J Robinson, R D Elders, E D Lofthouse, D Wardell, J Parkinson, A Thompson
Area	The civil parishes of Bradbury, Bishop Middleham, Cornforth, Fishburn, Mordon, Sedgefield and Trimdon in County Durham
Meets	In March and October each year, however urgent issues can be dealt with in between meetings.

Policy
The Sedgefield Charities comprises two charities, now the Sedgefield District Relief in Need Charity (No. 230392) and Howle Hope Estate (No. 230409), derived from similar charitable endowments dating from the eighteenth century.

The Trustees can provide relief in need grants to individuals or to other charitable bodies providing the same sort of relief within the area of benefit. Small grants are also made to local groups providing social facilities for the elderly and disabled.

Grants
- Sedgefield Pop-In Club - £5,010
- Fishburn Skills Centre - £3,000
- Sedgefield First Responders - £500
- Cornforth Youth Action Council – £500
- Sedgefield Guides - £500

Applications
Applications are by letter to the correspondent; referrals from Social Services etc. are in order. Applications from organisation should be accompanied by a business plan and, where the organisation is older than one year, the Trustees Report and Financial Statements (unaudited accounts may be presented). The Trustees of the Charities may seek further information.

Exclusions
Grants **cannot** be made to national, regional, borough or district charities unless it can be shown that the expenditure can be directly related to (an) inhabitant(s) of the area of benefit.

Shaftoe Educational Foundation

Correspondent	J P Richardson The Office Shaftoe Terrace Haydon Bridge Hexham NE47 6BW
Telephone	01434 684 298
CC No	528101
Income	£128,157 (2001)
Grants	No information given
Trustees	T A Bates, J W Clarkson, Mrs L A Philp, Mrs L A Gilhespy, Mrs E Garrow, T J Stephenson
Area	Haydon
Meets	March, July and November

Policy
The Foundation did not provide up to date information. The entry is based upon information held on the Charity Commission database and additional FINE research.

The Foundation funds local organisations and individuals for educational purposes in the Haydon area.

Grants
Grants range from £30 - £2,000.

Applications
In writing to the correspondent.

Exclusions
Anyone outside the Haydon area.

Shears Charitable Trust

Correspondent	The Trustee 35 Elmfield Road Gosforth Newcastle upon Tyne NE3 4BA
Telephone	0191 285 7523
CC No	1049907
Income	£167,773 (2000/01)
Grants	No information given
Trustees	L G Shears, T H Shears, P J R Shears
Area	Northumberland, Tyne & Wear & Durham
Meets	No information given

Policy
The Trust did not provide up to date information. The entry is based upon information held on the Charity Commission database and additional FINE research.

The Trust funds registered charities working within the following areas:
- Education / Training
- Medical / Health
- Disability
- Relief of poverty
- Overseas aid / famine relief
- Arts / Culture
- Environment / Conservation / Heritage
- Community development / Employment.

Grants
The Trust provides one-off grants up to a maximum of £5,000, although £1,000 is the typical grant size.

Shears Charitable Trust (Cont..)

Applications
In writing to the correspondent.

Exclusions
Animals.

Helpful Hint...

If a trust gives a phone number, use it to find out if they have guidelines available, what elements they usually / rarely consider and when the next deadline for applications is.

Sherburn House Charity

Correspondent	Stephen P. Hallett The Administration Office Ramsey House Sherburn Hospital Durham DH1 2SE
Telephone	0191 372 2551
Fax	0191 372 0035
E-mail	sphallett@sherburnhouse.org
Website	www.sherburnhouse.org
CC No	217652
Income	£1,913,000 (2002)
Grants	£500,000 per annum
Trustees	Rev Canon G Miller, Mrs M Bozic, Mrs W Brooks, Cllr S Laverick, Cllr D Forbes, Mrs D Gibson, Miss D J Hale, Mrs M R Hawgood, Mr G Hill, Mr L Perks, Dr G E Rodmell, Miss M L Rushford, Cllr L B Smith, Mr I Stewart, Cllr P Thompson, Mr R Wilson, Cllr. W Firby
Area	North East of England between the Scottish border and the River Tees
Meets	Every two months

Sherburn House Charity (Cont..)

Policy
The objects of the Trust are the relief of need, hardship and distress and therefore fairly wide. The Trust also makes grants to individuals (totalling approximately £180,000 per year – further details in the North East Guide to Grants for Individuals). The Trustees will consider funding work in the following categories:
• Health
• Mental Health
• Learning Disabilities
• Physically Disabled
• Substance Abuse
• Homelessness
• Special Needs
• Community Needs
• Effects of Long Term Unemployment.

Groups do not have to be registered charities to apply.

Grants
From April 2001 to March 2002 the charity has awarded 112 grants, totalling £581,428 – grants awarded ranged from £350 to £34,000.

Applications
Contact the Trust to be sent their application form. You should complete this and return it along with a copy of your latest accounts and annual report.

Exclusions
• Organisations which have substantial reserves or are in serious deficit
• Grant making bodies seeking to distribute funds on the charity's behalf
• Activities which are the responsibility of Central / Local Government or other statutory bodies
• Fabric appeals for places of worship per se
• Fabric appeals for halls except those which demonstrate service of activities for the whole community
• Fundraising events or activities
• General appeals
• Sponsorship
• Expeditions or overseas travel
• Mainstream educational activity
• National charities except those which have a strong representation within the charity's beneficial area
• Hospitals and medical centres (except hospices)
• Retrospective grants
• Applications from organisations who have received a grant or have been refused a grant within the preceding 2 years
• Those who do not fully complete the application form.

SITA Environmental Trust

Correspondent	Andrew Saunders Operations Manager The Barn Brinkmarsh Lane Falfield S Gloucestershire GL12 8PT
Telephone	01454 262910
Fax	01454 269090

Email
env-trust@sita.co.uk

Website
www.sitaenvtrust.co.uk

Income	£10,000,000 (2001)
Grants	£2,947,090 (2001)
Trustees	R Acock, G Eduljee, D Fitzsimons, M Gordon, J Leaver, K Reynolds
Area	UK
Meets	Every 8 weeks

Policy
(Incorporates Northumbria Water Environmental Trust (NWET) Fund) Funding is directed into two areas:

Sustainable Waste Management
These projects may involve R&D, recycling or education/promotion initiatives and can take place anywhere in the UK.

Community Projects
• Projects that create or maintain public parks and amenities. These

must be within a 10-mile radius of an active SITA landfill site.

• Projects that restore or repair buildings of religious worship or buildings of architectural or historic interest. These must be within a 3-mile radius of an active SITA landfill site.

Grants
Grants are usually between £1,000 and £1,000,000. Grants awarded in the North East in 2002:
• St Andrew's Church, Gateshead - £14,000 (restoration work)
• Birdisperse, Tyne & Wear - £17,000 (R&D project for discouraging birds at landfill sites)
• Durham Wildlife Services - £52,000 (habitat preservation)
• Northumbria Environmental Partnership - £30,000 (R&D project).

The Trust is also funding national programmes of work that benefits the North East including:
• Eco-Schools – a UK wide environmental education programme.
• Renew – white goods recycling and training for people with learning difficulties.

Applications
In writing to the correspondent.

Exclusions
Projects that **do not** conform with Entrust's guidelines. (ENTRUST is the regulator of the landfill tax credit scheme).

The Henry Smith Charity

Correspondent   c/o Jane Shewell
Grants Director
Community
Foundation
Percy House
Percy Street
Newcastle upon Tyne
NE1 4PW

Telephone   0191 222 0945

Fax   0191 230 0689

Email
js@communityfoundation.org.uk

Website
www.henrysmithcharity.org.uk
/www.communityfoundation.org.uk

CC No   230102

Grants   £496,280 (2001)
(within the North
East)

Area   United Kingdom.

Meets   March, June,
September,
December

Policy
The Charity works in partnership in the North East region with the Community Foundation. The Foundation recommends a small number of applications in the North East to The Henry Smith Charity. The criteria for selecting grants are:

- To fund innovatory projects, which may have an element of risk and which have a reasonable chance of continuing if successful.
- To provide further funding for new projects that have proved their worth and are unable to obtain support from other sources.
- To fund voluntary organisations with potential for further development, possibly because of new management or new service opportunities.
- To provide core funding for established organisations which are either exemplary projects or support a range of initiatives in their field.

Grants can be for revenue or capital projects. The Trustees use the following categories to classify grants:
- Community service
- Counselling and family services
- Disability
- Drugs and alcohol
- Elderly
- Holidays for disabled and poor children
- Homeless
- Hospices and palliative care
- Hospitals and medical care
- Medical research
- Young people.

Applicants should show how the work will be sustained thereafter as The Henry Smith Charity only occasionally makes continuation grants.

Grants are made to registered charities, but in exceptional circumstances may be made through the Community Foundation to an organisation in the process of registering.

Successful applicants are required to submit two written reports per year outlining progress with key tasks agreed with Community Foundation staff and detailing agreed outcomes. Community Foundation staff make annual review visits.

The Henry Smith Charity (Cont..)

<u>Small Grants Programme:</u> Applications for the Charity's small grant programme can be submitted directly to the Charity at any time during the year and are considered fortnightly between January and December. All applications received which are within the Charity's objects and policy will be considered. The programme is available to organisations with an annual income of under £250,000. Grants can be for capital or revenue purposes. However on-going running costs are unlikely to be supported as grants need to be spent within a six-month period.

Grants
The Charity awarded 19 grants through the Community Foundation to North East organisations in 2001/2002, totalling, £496,280. Grants range from £10,000 to £100,000 (over three years).

FINE has a full list of grants made. Examples include:
- Children North East - £40,000 per year for three years to fund the Sherburn Road Children's Initiative in Durham.
- Cleveland Housing Advice Centre - £14,000 for running costs of a volunteer advice project
- Berwick Family Centre - £45,000 for core revenue costs
- Wansbeck Toy Library - £15,000 per year for three years staff costs.

The Small Grants Programme makes grants of between £500 and £10,000.

Applications
Applications for larger grants are made via the Community Foundation using the Foundation's application form. Any organisation wishing to apply to the Charity is requested to enquire at the Community Foundation before submitting an application, which should be sent to the Community Foundation.

The applications are then considered by the Trustees of The Henry Smith Charity who have sole responsibility for making a grant. Applications from the North East are considered on merit in competition with applications submitted to the Charity from across the UK.

It can take up to six months from first discussion with the Community Foundation to final decision by the Charity.

Voluntary organisations in the North East may also apply directly to The Henry Smith Charity. The Community Foundation aims to research and recommend applications but not act as the sole "gatekeeper" on applications to the Charity.

The Small Grants Programme does not require an application form, applications are made in writing direct to the Trustees.

Guidelines are available by contacting the Charity sending an A4 SAE with stamps to the value of 41p (1st) or 33p (2nd), or visiting the website. The address is as follows; The Treasurer, The Henry Smith Charity, 5 Chancery Lane, Clifford's Inn, London, EC4A 1BU. Tel: 020 7242 1212.

Exclusions
The Charity does **not** make grants to or for the following:
- Arts projects
- Church buildings
- Education projects
- Environmental projects
- Individuals
- Large capital appeals (unless most of the funding has been raised)
- Leisure projects.

Smith (Haltwhistle & District) Charitable Trust

Correspondent	J Y Luke Secretary Sun Alliance House 35 Mosley Street Newcastle upon Tyne NE1 1XX
CC No	200520
Income	No information available
Grants	£34,110 (1996/97)
Trustees	I M Smith, Dr F G Pattrick, Dr R A D Pattrick, J M Clark, Rev R B Cook, N C C Clayburn
Area	The North East of England, primarily Northumberland
Meets	Once a year, in July

Policy
The Trust did not respond to requests for information therefore the entry is based on information previously held by FINE.

Grants are made to local organisations and charities in the North East as well as to national charities operating in the area. More than half of the Trust's funds go to regular beneficiaries.

Grants
In the year ending 31 July 1997, the Trust made 83 grants (57 to regular beneficiaries), totalling £34,110. All grants, except one, were for less than £1,000.

Applications
In writing to the correspondent.

Exclusions
No grants are made to individuals except through a specific charity.

Helpful Hint...

Reread your application carefully before posting it, to make sure you haven't left anything out or made any mistakes, as this damages your credibility – even better get someone else to do it !

Bernard Sunley Charitable Foundation

Correspondent	Dr. Brian Martin Director 4th Floor 20 Berkeley Square London W1J 6LH
CC No	269109
Telephone	020 7408 2198
Fax	020 7499 5859
Income	£3,564,000 (1997)
Grants	£2,772,058 (1997)
Trustees	J B Sunley, J M Tice, B Sunley, Sir D Gosling
Area	Worldwide
Meets	Quarterly

Policy

The Foundation did not respond to requests, for information therefore the entry is based on information previously held by FINE.

The income of the Foundation is to be applied in giving grants to such charitable institutions as the Trustees in their absolute discretion may select.

In 1997/98, the total awarded to various categories of charities was:
- Community Aid and Recreation - £774,165
- The Arts, Museums etc - £105,180
- Universities, Colleges and Schools - £379,810
- General Medicine - £105,700
- Youth Clubs, Youth Training and Sports Organisations - £238,400
- Hospitals, Medical Schools and Research - £385,575
- Provision for the Elderly, including Housing - £277,688
- Wildlife and the Environment - £81,700
- Overseas - £178,515
- Churches and Chapels - £106,050
- Professional and Public Bodies and Miscellaneous - £61,625
- Service Charities - £77,650.

Grants

More than 2,000 applications were received, from which 300 grants were made, totalling £2,772,058. Grants ranged from under £1,000 to £200,000.

There was only one North East grant disclosed in the Trustees Report for the year ending 5 April 1998:
- Wallsend Sea Cadet Corps., North Tyneside - £4,000.

Applications

The Foundation does not publish guidelines for applicants, nor does it use an application form.

Written applications should be sent to the correspondent and must always be supported by a copy of the latest audited accounts or "independently examined accounts" as applicable. The most recent Annual Report should also be included. The letter should give details as to the following points:
- What the charity is, what it does and what its objectives are (quoting the registered charity number).
- Describe the project for which the grant is required. Explain the need for the project and its purpose. Who will benefit and how?

Bernard Sunley Charitable Foundation (Cont..)

- How much will the project cost? This costing should be itemised and supported (quotations etc) as necessary.
- What size of grant is requested?
- How much has been raised and from whom?
- How is the applicant planning to raise the shortfall?

If applicable, show how the on-going running costs of the project will be met once the project is established. Any other documentation that the applicant feels will help to support or explain their case.

No reply is given to unsuccessful applicants.

Exclusions
Grants are only made to registered charities. No grants to individuals.

Teesside Emergency Relief Fund

Correspondent	Tanya Harrison Secretary to the Trustees Law and Democracy Stockton Borough Council Municipal Buildings Church Road Stockton-on-Tees TS18 1LD
Telephone	01642 393 070
Fax	01642 393 076

E-mail
tanya.harrison@stockton.gov.uk

Income	No information given
Grants	No information given
Trustees	The Worshipful The Mayor of Stockton, Director of Law and Democracy, Stockton-on-Tees Borough Council, Corporate Director of Resources
Area	Former County of Teesside (i.e. Middlesbrough, Redcar, Stockton, Thornaby, Billingham and Eston)
Meets	Usually monthly

Policy
The Fund aims to relieve either generally or individually persons who are in conditions of need, hardship or

Teesside Emergency Relief Fund (Contd...)

distress by: making grants of money, making interest free loans, providing or paying for items, services or facilities which will reduce the need, hardship or distress of such persons.

The majority of grants that are made are for household items for people who are considered by the Trustees to be in extreme specific need or hardship, for either a social or medical reason.

Grants have also been awarded to disabled individuals who require items that would enable them to live more independently. The Trustees have also assisted charitable organisations who provide assistance to such people providing they reside within the Trust Fund area.

Applicants must reside within the former Teesside County Borough which was set up in 1968, this includes the county borough of Middlesbrough, the non-county boroughs of Redcar, Stockton and Thornaby and the urban districts of Billingham and Eston.

In exceptional circumstances, the Trustees can grant relief to persons immediately outside the area of benefit who, in the opinion of the Trustees, ought to be treated as if they were residents within the area. The requirements for receiving an award are as follows:

- Each item applied for must be required for a specific need or be calculated to reduce or relieve some specific hardship or distress e.g. social or medical
- All applications must be accompanied by a supporting letter from either the applicant's Social Worker, Health Visitor, Welfare Officer, GP, Probation Officer, Local Tenancy Services

Officer, Citizens Advice Bureau or a representative of any other appropriate professional body
- Proof of income must be supplied by the applicant, the applicant's partner and / or those receiving income on behalf of the household. Please provide photocopies of the notification of benefit, benefit books or payslip if employed
- In the event of the organisation you approached in order to provide a supporting letter being unable to take responsibility for monitoring the application of any award made, please name a shop from which you would be able to purchase the items requested on the form. If an award is made, vouchers will be issued to you from your chosen shop.

Grants
During the year ending 31 March 1998, the following grants were made to organisations:
- Scope, Teesside - £1,745 to purchase equipment for members
- British Red Cross - £2,000 towards refurbishment of their centre in Thornaby
- Cleveland Community Foundation - £10,000 as matched funding.

Applications
Guidelines and application forms are available from the correspondent.

Exclusions
Grants **will not** be awarded:
- To relieve rates, taxes, other public funds or payment of existing loans or debts
- To pay or contribute towards the cost of holidays or associated costs
- To pay for any non-essential electrical goods, such as televisions, video recorders,

Teesside Emergency Relief Fund (Contd..)

stereo equipment, telephones etc. (except in extreme cases)
- To pay for items such as cookers when means of cooking / heating food already exist
- To replace household items that could be preserved with the correct prevention and attention
- To replace mattresses damaged due to bedwetting.

The Trustees must assess the application on the basis of the perceived extent of the applicant's need and the relevance of the requested items in meeting that need, together with priority of the request. The Trustees' decision is made on the information provided; no further explanation can be offered once the decision has been made.

TFM Cash Challenge Appeal

Correspondent	Tracey Butler Secretary TFM Radio Yale Crescent Thornaby Stockton-On-Tees TS17 6AA
CC No	1065727
Telephone	01642 888 222
Fax	01642 868 288
Email	radio@tfm.ace.co.uk
Income	£11,794 (1997/98)
Grants	£10,410 (1997/98)
Trustees	Committee of members of the public not connected to the radio station
Area	TFM broadcasting area (Teesside, North Yorkshire, and the south of County Durham, bounded by Peterlee)
Meets	Twice a year, usually January and July/August

Policy
The Trust did not respond to requests for information therefore the entry is based on information previously held by FINE.

TFM raises money throughout the year, involving a variety of on and off air fund-raising events, to provide money for specific capital projects or

TFM Cash Challenge Appeal (Cont...)

pieces of equipment. It is intended that the appeal should benefit a large number of local people, therefore organisations will be supported, rather than applications on behalf of individuals or very small groups.

Applicants must be local groups or active local branches of national charities. Groups should be unable to purchase the equipment or fund the project from either existing funds or foreseeable income.

The beneficiaries should be unable to meet the identified need themselves. The majority of grants are between £100 and £3,000.

Grants
In the year ending 24/4/98, the appeal awarded 15 grants, totalling £10,410. Grants ranged from £50 to £2,460.

Applications
Guidelines and application forms are available from the correspondent.

Exclusions
See policy.

The Baily Thomas Charitable Fund

Correspondent	Mr G P Mean Ernst & Young LLP 400 Capability Green Luton Beds LU1 3LU
CC No	262334
Income	£3,242,463 (2001)
Grants	£2,848,959 (2001)
Trustees	Charles Jocelyn Tichborne Nangle, Michael Robert Macfadyen, Prof. Michael Graham Gelder, Prof. William Irvine Fraser CBE
Area	None specified
Meets	June and early December (the deadline for applications are, 1st May and 1st October respectively)

Policy
The Fund was established primarily to aid the research into learning disability and to aid the care and relief of those affected by learning disability by making grants to voluntary organisations working in this field.

Applications will only be considered from voluntary groups which are registered charities or are associated with a registered charity.

Funding is considered for capital and revenue costs and for both specific projects and general running / core costs.

The Baily Thomas Charitable Fund (Cont..)

Grants are normally one-off awards but exceptionally a new pilot project may be funded over 2 to 3 years subject to satisfactory reports of progress.

The following areas of work normally fall within the Fund's policy:
- Capital building / renovation / refurbishment works for residential, nursing and respite care and schools
- Employment schemes including woodwork, crafts, printing and horticulture
- Play schemes and play therapy schemes
- Day and social activities including: building costs and running costs; support for families including respite schemes
- Independent living schemes
- Swimming and hydro-therapy pools and snoezelen rooms.

Grants

Among the top 50 grants awarded by the Fund in the year ending 30th September 2001 were:
- Bliss=Ability - £50,000, to provide information services in the Tyne & Wear area
- Percy Hedley Foundation - £15,000 towards the conversion and refurbishment of a school.

Applications

Applications should be made on the Fund's standard application form. Forms and guidelines for applicants are available from the correspondent.

All applications to the Fund will be subject to independent review.

A copy of the latest annual report and accounts must be enclosed with the application form.

Do not send architectural drawings, plans or photographs – these are seldom necessary and will be requested if required.

Where a specific project is funded, successful applicants will normally be asked to submit a brief, written report on completion of the project.

A second application from an organisation will not normally be considered for a period of at least one year after completion of an initial grant or notification of an unsuccessful application.

Exclusions

The Fund **does not** normally support:
- Hospices
- Minibuses (except those for residential and / or day care services for the learning disabled)
- Advocacy projects
- Arts and theatre projects
- Physical disabilities unless accompanied by significant learning disabilities.

Individuals **will not** be funded.

Thompson's of Prudhoe Environmental Trust

Correspondent	Colin Basey Project Director Princess Way Low Prudhoe Northumberland NE42 6PL
CC No	1064360
Income	£653,293 (2000)
Grants	£1,536,361 (2000)
Trustees	G I Holmes, J Thompson, P McCarron, M Smith, J Bessell
Area	The company operate landfill sites at Thornbrough (Northumberland), Springwell (Tyne & Wear), Bishop Middleham and Barmpton (both in County Durham). Projects must be within 10 miles of a site.
Meets	Quarterly

Policy

The Trust has been established to distribute funds received from Thompson's of Prudhoe Ltd under the Landfill Tax Credit Scheme. The Trust can support projects which meet one or more of the objects set out in the Landfill Tax Regulations 1996, including:

- Reclamation and restoration of land for economic, social or environmental use where it has been prevented or restricted because of previous use.
- Any operation intended to prevent or reduce any potential for pollution or to remedy or mitigate the effects of any pollution on land polluted by a previous activity.
- Encourage the use of more sustainable waste management practices, through research and development, education or collection and dissemination of information on such practices where it is for the protection of the environment, the provision, maintenance or improvement of a public park or other public amenity in the vicinity of a landfill site or the maintenance, repair or restoration of a building or other structure which is a place of religious worship or of historic or architectural interest.

The Small Grants Programme will consider applications for project funding up to £5,000. Those over £5,000 will be considered under the Main Grants Programme.

Grants

The Trust awarded 174 grants, totalling £1,536,361, in the year ending 28 February 2001.
FINE has a full list of all grants made – the following are some examples:

- Action for Blind People - £1,000
- Balliol Youth Centre Longbenton - £2,000
- Berwick Mind - £500
- Childline Yorkshire & North East - £500
- Diocese of Newcastle - £250
- Eastgate Village Hall Durham - £1,000
- Faramir Trust - £250
- Gateway Club Hexham - £250
- Lady Hoare Trust - £1,000
- MENCAP - £250
- NCTC - £2,500

Thompson's of Prudhoe Environmental Trust (Cont..)

- Northumberland County Scout Council - £2,000
- Riverside Netball Club - £100
- South Tyneside Stroke Club - £250
- The Outdoor Trust Northumberland - £500
- Wheels Project South Shields - £1,000
- YMCA Newcastle - £5,000.

Applications
There is an application form for the Small Grants Programme, which is available from the correspondent. Guidelines for the Main Grants Programme are also available.

Applications may be submitted at any time, but should reach the correspondent at least 4 weeks before the next board meeting (these take place in mid January, April, July and October).

Applications may take 4 months or longer to be turned round.

Exclusions
None specified in the guidelines, however proposals must have an environmental slant and must come within one or more of the categories detailed in Policy, with particular emphasis on the first three points highlighted in Policy.

The Tubney Charitable Trust

Correspondent	Mrs Catherine Small Administrator C/O Nabarro Nathanson The Anchorage 34 Bridge Street Reading RG1 2LU
Telephone	0118 925 4662
Fax	0118 950 5640

E-mail
c.small@nabarro.com

Website
www.tubney.org.uk

CC No	1061480
Income	£26,696,599 (01/02)
Grants	£550,577 (01/02)
Trustees	Jonathan Burchfield, Terry Collins, Jim Kennedy, René Olivieri
Area	UK and overseas
Meets	Quarterly, end of April, July, October and January

Policy
The Trust reformed during 2001 and as such no accounts for the previous financial period are available.
The Trust's general policy will be to support UK registered, exempt and excepted charities which undertake charitable activities where there is a demonstrable element of outward provision and benefit to the community at large. Grants available

The Tubney Charitable Trust (Cont..)

are between £30,000 and £250,000 per funding year.

Grants will be made in relation to both capital and revenue costs.

The Trustees will consider applications falling within the following categories:

The Natural Environment
The Trustees wish to support environmental charities which are associated with the conservation of the natural environment.

Animal Welfare and Conservation
The Trustees wish to support charities associated with animal welfare and alleviating animal suffering. Although the focus will be mainly farm and domestic animals, the Trust will also consider supporting non-domestic animal welfare. The Trustees also wish to support charities concerned with the conservation of endangered species. Grants will be made for projects which:

- Relieve the distress and suffering of animals and promote animal welfare; or
- Preserve rare breeds and protect endangered species.

The Promotion of Access for the Disadvantaged (primarily the disabled) to Education and the Arts
Support under this programme is available to charities that promote access for the disadvantaged (primarily those with physical or learning disabilities) to education and the arts.

Palliative Care
The Trustees wish to support charities providing palliative care and support for those suffering from life-threatening illnesses, and their families.

Grants
Grants have been to organisations working within areas such as:
- Hospices
- Wildlife Trusts / Animal Rescue
- Disabilities
- Education.

Applications
Application is by completion of the Trust's application form. The latest audited or independently examined accounts must be included.

The closing dates for applications are: 31st March, 30th June, 30th September and 31st December.

Whenever possible, applicants will be notified of the Trustees' decision within 6 months of the close of the relevant application period.

The receipt of all applications is acknowledged and all applicants will hear whether their application has been successful.

If the application is unsuccessful the applicant may not re-apply for the same project within 12 months of submitting the first application, but may apply for other projects at any time.

Exclusions
The Tubney Charitable Trust **will not** generally make grants to:
- Individuals
- Non-UK charities (although grants may be made to UK charities operating overseas)
- Housing / homelessness charities
- Refugees
- Non-specific university appeals
- Projects that replace statutory funding and provision
- Retrospective funding

The Tubney Charitable Trust (Cont..)

- The promotion of sectarian religious interests
- Large national charities which already enjoy widespread public support
- Projects / work which cannot demonstrate a sufficiently wide degree of public access
- The repair and maintenance of historic buildings or the funding of new buildings, other than where such building works fall within another programme
- Medical research
- Pure research, publications, public lectures or the development of websites.

Helpful Hint...

Always endeavours to find the name of the Trust Secretary / person to whom you are applying. It looks more personal than "To whom it may concern".

The Tudor Trust

Correspondent	The Trustees 7 Ladbroke Grove London W11 3BD
Telephone	020 7727 8522
Fax	020 7221 8522
CC No	206260
Income	£12,727,000 (01/02)
Grants	£22,634,000 (01/02)
Trustees	Grove Charity Management Limited
Area	Mainly within the UK
Meets	Continuously throughout the year

Policy:

The Tudor Trust makes grants to charities and organisations with charitable objectives. Support is given both for capital and revenue costs. The Trustees decide which charitable purposes are not to be funded. A full policy review is undertaken every three years. The next review is due 2003/2004.

The Trust is selective in what it supports within relatively broad areas of activity. Demand for funding greatly exceeds available resources and not all applications meeting the current criteria will be successful. Grants are given from £500 upwards. Loans are offered occasionally. Applications may be sent at any time to the Trustees.

The Trustees are keen to support organisations and groups which help people to fulfil their potential and make a positive contribution to the

The Tudor Trust (Cont..)

communities in which they live. The Trust will focus its funding where there is a significant need in both rural and urban communities.

Schemes addressing rural isolation will receive special consideration. Projects which offer accessible, integrated and sustained support to people who are vulnerable or only just managing are of particular interest.

The Trust will target projects working alongside young people (9-18 years old), families and older people living in disadvantaged or marginalised communities.

Organisations whose main focus of work incorporates **at least** one of the following areas of work can be considered for funding:
* Accommodation
* Education
* Health
* Recreation
* Relationships
* Resources.

The Trust particularly wants to fund projects developing services with:
* People with mental health problems and head injuries.
* People who are substance misusers.
* People who are homeless.
* Offenders/ex-offenders, people at risk of re-offending (and their families).
* People at risk.

The Trust's guidelines set out the criteria in more detail.

Grants

FINE has a full list of grants made to organisations in the North East of England during 2000/2001, the following are examples:

* Walker Health Project - £105,000
* Bishop Auckland Community Partnership - £100,000
* East Cleveland Youth Housing Initiative - £42,000
* Hartlepool Alzheimer's Trust - £30,000
* Fawdon Community Association - £20,000
* Hexham Youth Initiative - £20,000
* Springwell Village Hall Association - £7,000
* Consett Churches Detached Youth Project - £4,000
* Durham Action on Single Housing - £4,000.

Applications

The leaflet "How to Apply" is available from the Trust office, or on the Trust's website.

Applications can only be made in writing and should include:
* A summary of the current work of the organisation with the latest annual report.
* A description of the project / proposal / area of work for which funding is required.
* An indication of the numbers of people involved / likely to be involved and how they will benefit.
* A breakdown of costs.
* Details of funding raised or committed to date and steps being taken to raise the balance.
* Any other relevant information such as catchment area served, numbers attending existing activities. Drawings or plans are helpful for new buildings or major refurbishments.
* The latest annual accounts or a copy of a recent financial statement if the organisation is newly formed.

Applications can be sent at any time to the correspondent. The assessment process can take up to 8 weeks once all relevant information is received.

The Tudor Trust (Cont..)

Please do not telephone for news of progress during this period. Ineligible applicants will be told almost immediately.

Organisations are requested not to re-apply to the Trust for at least 12 months after a grant has been awarded or an application has been unsuccessful.

Exclusions

The following areas are unlikely to receive funding:
- People with learning disabilities
- People with physical disabilities
- People with physical illnesses.

These areas are outside the current guidelines and cannot be considered for funding:
- Activity centres
- Advice
- Advocacy
- After school clubs
- Animal charities
- Arts
- Breakfast clubs
- Bursaries and scholarships
- Capacity building and technical support
- Church and hall fabric appeals
- Colleges
- Commercial organisations
- Community foundations
- Community transport
- Conferences/seminars
- Councils for Voluntary Service
- Counselling
- Disabilities (mental and physical)
- Endowment appeals
- Expeditions/overseas travel
- Fabric
- Fundraising events/salaries of fundraisers
- Halls and Church centres

- Helplines
- Holiday/holiday centres
- Homework clubs
- Illness (physical)
- Individuals
- Large national charities enjoying widespread support
- Leisure clubs
- Medical care
- Mother tongue classes/cultural activities
- Museums/places of entertainment
- Neighbourhood mediation
- Nurseries, crèches, pre-school childcare
- Play schemes and groups, parent and toddler groups
- Playgrounds
- Research
- Religion
- Schools
- Sponsorship and marketing appeals
- Training and employment schemes
- Uniformed organisations
- Universities
- Victims (of crime, domestic and sexual abuse, trauma, war)
- Volunteer centres
- Women's centres.

Tyneside Charitable Trust

Correspondent	Mr S Lamb 43 Fairfield Drive Cullercoats North Shields Tyne and Wear NE30 3AG
Telephone	0191 252 0663
CC No	505758
Income	£25,388 (2001)
Grants	£25,250 (2001)
Trustees	R H Dickinson, R A Dickinson
Area	North of England, particularly North Tyneside
Meets	Once a year in November

Policy
The money to endow the Trust came from Swan Hunters to be used for the relief of former employees of the company and its subsidiaries, or their dependents, and also to charitable organisations at the discretion of the Trustees.

Most of the income is distributed to a group of charities on a regular list, mainly for medical research and youth organisations. A few other grants are awarded each year. In 2001 grants awarded ranged from £500 to £2,500.

Grants
The grants awarded in 2001 totalled £25,250, as follows:
- Northumberland Association of Clubs for Young People - £1,500
- Soldiers, Sailors and Airmen's Families Association - £1,000
- St Oswald's Hospice - £2,500
- Mental Health Foundation - £1,000
- Age Concern, North Shields - £1,500
- Samaritans of Tyneside - £1,000
- Newcastle Council for Disabled - £500
- Sea Cadet Corps - £500
- Northern Counties School for the Deaf – £750
- National Lifeboat Institutes – £500
- Iris Fund for the prevention of Blindness- £500
- Northumberland Scout Association - £500
- Marie Curie Memorial Foundation - £2,000
- Northumberland Deaf Mission - £1,500
- Alzheimer's Disease Society - £1,250
- Breathe North - £750
- Macmillan Nurses - £1,000
- Red Cross Northumbria - £2,000
- HMS Trincomalee Trust - £1,000
- Child Bereavement Trust - £5,000

Applications
Apply in writing to the correspondent.

Exclusions
No grants are awarded to individuals.

The Vardy Foundation

Correspondent	Sir Peter Vardy Chair of Trustees Houghton House Emperor Way Doxford International Business Park Sunderland SR3 3XR
CC No	328415
Income	£1,092,954 (2000)
Grants	No information given
Trustees	Sir P Vardy, Mrs M B Vardy, R A R Vardy
Area	UK
Meets	No information given

Policy
The Trust did not respond to requests for information the entry therefore is based upon by FINE research and the Charity Commission Database.
The Trust makes grants to organisations with charitable purposes particularly those involved with education and Christianity. The Trust supports organisations that have a particular interest in the North East of England.

Grants
Grants have been made to Church organisations, hospitals and educational institutions. The grants awarded range is size from £100 to £100,000.

Applications
In writing to the correspondent.

Exclusions
No information given.

Wallsend Charitable Trust

Correspondent	North Tyneside Council Marine House Norman Terrace Willington Quay Tyne & Wear NE28 6SU
Telephone	0191 200 7046
CC No	215476
Income	£59,165 (1999)
Grants	£18,365 (1999)
Trustees	Cllr M Huscroft, B Springthorne, Ms S Watson, Cllr D Charlton, Cllr T Cruikshanks, Cllr M Mulgrove, Cllr R Usher Mrs M Kelly, Mrs M Lavery
Area	Wallsend
Meets	Quarterly (March, June, September and December)

Policy
The Trust did not respond to requests for information therefore the entry is based upon FINE research.

The Trust funds individuals and local organisations benefitting older people, and people who are disadvantaged by poverty or homelessness.

Grants
No information given.

Applications
Application forms are available from the correspondent.

Wallsend Charitable Trust (Cont..)

Successful applicants are required to wait for 12 months before re-applying.

It is not generally worthwhile for unsuccessful applicants to re-apply.

Exclusions
Organisations outside Wallsend.

Helpful Hint...

You need to think about how you will measure your success – how will you report this back to your funders?

Washington Community Development Trust

Correspondent	R G Wilson Secretary 60 John F Kennedy Estate Washington Tyne & Wear NE38 7AJ
CC No	511134
Income	£7,162 (2000)
Grants	No information given
Trustees	S Arbuckle, M Murphy, R Wilson, I Gray, R Muncaster, T Gauntlet, Cllr B Craddock, P Dawson, M Wilson, R Boom, L Brewin.
Area	Washington
Meets	Monthly

Policy
The Trust did not respond to requests for information the entry therefore is based upon information previously held by FINE and additional research.

The Trust prefers to support new groups/organisations in the Washington area, by giving one-off grants. Grants are given to groups/organisations who will benefit the area.

Grants
Grants range from £50 - £500.
Grants are available to:
* Credit Unions
* Music Groups
* Residents Association
* Youth Clubs.

**Washington Community
Development Trust (Cont..)**

Applications
In writing to the correspondent.

Exclusions
Grants are not given for events.

The Weavers Company Benevolent Fund

Correspondent	Mr J R Snowdon
Saddlers' House
Gutter Lane
London
EC2V 6BR
Telephone	020 7606 1155
Fax	020 7606 1119
Website	www.charity@weaversco.co.uk/
CC No	266189
Income	No information given
Grants	£162,533 (2001)
Trustees	The Court of Assistants of the Company at any one time
Area	UK
Meets	February, June and October

Policy
The Worshipful Company of Weavers awards one-off grants and recurrent grants to a maximum of three years, preferring to support small or new community-based organisations, where the grants would form a substantial part of the funding.

The Worshipful Company of Weavers are particularly interested in supporting innovative projects in their early stages, especially those that can be evaluated and may act as a catalyst for other work elsewhere.

The areas of particular interest to the Trust are:

The Weavers Company Benevolent Fund (Cont..)

- Young people at risk of criminal involvement
- Young offenders
- The rehabilitation of prisoners and ex-prisoners.

The grants provided can be used towards capital items, organisation running costs, project revenue costs and building work.
Grants are only available to registered charities or organisations applying for charitable status.

Grants
No information supplied.

Applications
Guidelines for applicants are available from the Trust. The initial application should be made by letter and give information about the organisation together with:

- A clear, concise outline of the work for which funding is being sought
- A budget for the proposed project
- A copy of the latest annual report and accounts.

All applicants will be informed about the outcome of their application. Unsuccessful applicants are required to wait for 12 months before re-applying for grants.

Successful applicants are required to provide the Trust with regular progress reports including statistical information, where appropriate, for evaluation purposes.

Exclusions
The Worshipful Company of Weavers is **not able** to provide:

- Funding for general appeals
- Funding for work that does not fit into the Trust's areas of interest

- Funding for running costs or deficit funding for established projects
- Replacement funding for grants etc. provided by statutory or other charitable trusts
- Funding for individuals, or for large, well-established charities
- Long term funding.

Helpful Hint...

Remember the funder is primarily interested in the need for what you are doing, not in your continuing existence.

The William Webster Charitable Trust

Correspondent	Miss M Bertenshaw Trust Officer Barclays Bank Trust Company Limited Osborne Court Gadbrook Park Northwich Cheshire CW9 7UE
Telephone	01606 313173
CC No	259848
Income	No information given
Grants	£74,300 (2001)
Trustees	Barclays Bank Trust Company Limited
Area	Northumberland, Tyne & Wear, Durham, the former county of Cleveland and the far north of Yorkshire
Meets	Three times a year in March, July and November

Policy
The Trust's general policy is to help "people rather than things" and in particular charities for youth, the elderly and disabled people; community organisations and health care projects are also supported. Whilst the Trust will support projects which also receive funds from the state, it is not prepared to consider crisis funding for revenue purposes or to replace statutory funding.

Grants are for capital costs and cannot be considered for day-to-day running costs.

Almost all grants are one-off, ranging from £250 to £5,000. The majority of grants are under £1,000.
The Trust is administered by Barclays Bank Trust Company Limited and is advised by a local advisory committee on the distribution of its funds.

Grants
The Trust made 61 grants during 2001, totalling £74,300. The smallest grant was for £250 and the largest for £2,800.
Grants include:
- Cornforth Youth Action Council - £500
- Durham Community Association - £500
- Hexham Canoe Club – Community Council of Northumberland - £250
- Shildon Methodist Church - £1,000
- Swaledale Outdoor Club – £2,000
- Women's Institute – Heddon on the Wall - £1,500
- Wylam First School PTA - £1,500.

Applications
Applications are in writing only and should include:
- Details of the project
- How much is required
- How much has already been raised from other sources
- A balance sheet.

You should also send your latest report and accounts.

Applications are not acknowledged.

Exclusions
No grants are made to individuals.

Garfield Weston Foundation

Correspondent	Fiona M. Hare Administrator Weston Centre Bowater House 68 Knightsbridge London SW1X 7LQ
Telephone	020 7589 6363
Fax	020 7584 5921
CC No	230260
Income	£54 million (2001)
Grants	£39 million (2001)
Trustees	G H Weston, Miriam Burnett, R Nancy Baron, Camilla Dalglish, W G Galen Weston, Jana Khayat, Anna Hobhouse, G Weston, Sophia Mason
Area	United Kingdom
Meets	Monthly

Policy
The Foundation has a generalist grant making policy. All applications are considered by the Trustees on an individual basis.

In the most recent annual report grants seem to be divided into the following categories: arts, community, education, environment, health, mental health, religion, welfare and youth.

One-off grants are given to registered charities and can be made for capital items, organisation running costs, project revenue costs and building work. Grants can be made to non-registered charities via an intermediary charity such as a Council for Voluntary Service.

Charities are asked not to re-apply within a twelve month period of an application to the Foundation, whether they have received a grant or not.

In assessing applications the Trustees take into consideration, amongst other things, the financial viability of the organisation, the degree of need for the project requiring funding and the ability of the organisation to achieve the goals.

Grants
The Foundation made 1,682 grants in the year ending April 2001 totalling £38,897,920. Grants ranged from £100 to £1,000,000. The total distribution by category was as follows:
- Arts - £3,800,500
- Community - £624,300
- Education - £13,503,200
- Environment - £2,277,000
- Health - £6,683,400
- Mental Health - £586,250
- Religion - £3,785,700
- Welfare - £4,959,450
- Youth - £2,045,620
- Other - £532,500.

188 grants were made to North East organisations, totalling £1,554,100. FINE has a full list of grants. Examples include:
- University of Sunderland Development Trust - £500,000
- Fawdon Community Association - £5,000
- Bede's World - £10,000
- Durham Wildlife Trust - £3,000
- Teeside Hospice Care Foundation - £3,000

Garfield Weston Foundation (cont..)

- Parish Church of St. Andrew - £5,000
- Byker Bridge Housing Association Ltd. - £5,000
- Millennium PHAB Club, Jarrow - £1,000
- Kids Kabin, Newcastle - £5,000
- Belle Vue Sports and Youth Centre, Hartlepool - £1,000
- Tynemouth District Scout Council - £1,000.

Applications

Apply in writing, including a brief description of the project together with an outline of the charity's activities, the charity's registration number, a copy of the most recent report and audited accounts, a financial plan and details of current and proposed fundraising.

Applications are initially screened by the Foundation staff to establish whether sufficient information has been submitted. Further details are sometimes requested before any further action is taken. A visit may also be arranged in order to gain a greater insight into an organisation.

The Foundation welcomes exploratory telephone calls from organisations considering making an application, to discuss the project.

Exclusions

Applications from or for the following are **not** considered:
- Organisations which do not have registered charitable status (see Policy details)
- Individuals
- Animal welfare
- Specific salary costs
- Organisations outside the UK.

1989 Willan Charitable Trust

Correspondent	Mr A Fettes Trustee 8 Kelso Drive The Priory's Tynemouth NE29 9NS
CC No	802749
Income	£615,277 (2000)
Grants	£505,400 (2000)
Trustees	E Willan, P R M Harbottle, A Fettes
Area	National and international, although in practice most grants are awarded in the North East (from Berwick to Hull)
Meets	Four times a year (usually in March, June, September and November)

Policy

The aims of the Trust are:
- To advance the education of children and to help children in need
- To encourage the study of animals and birds and their protection for the benefit of mankind
- To benefit aged, infirm, blind, deaf, crippled or mentally afflicted persons and alleviate hardship and distress suffered by any person or group or collection of persons
- To further medical research.

Grants

The Trust awarded 156 grants, totalling £505,400, in the year ending

1989 Willan Charitable Trust (Cont..)

November 2000. Grants ranged from £500 to £10,000 – the majority of donations are for £3,000.
Examples include:

- PDSA Newcastle - £3,000
- Downes Syndrome Association - £3,000
- 8th Whitley Bay Scouts - £3,000
- Sunderland Women's Centre - £3,000
- Jarrow Detached Youth Project - £3,000
- Tynedale Women's Training Group - £3,000
- Perth Green Community Association - £3,000
- Astley School Building Improvements - £5,000
- Heaton & Wallsend Methodist Church - £3,000
- Sargent Cancer Care for Children - £3,000
- Newcastle Society for the Blind - £3,000
- Newburn District Sea Cadets - £3,000
- Durham Action in Single Housing - £3,000
- North West Rhinos Wheelchair Rugby Group - £4,000
- St Patrick's Parents and Toddlers Group - £3,000.

Applications
Applications are in writing to the correspondent.

Exclusions
Grants are usually only made to registered charities (occasionally to non-registered charities via a CVS).

The Women's Trust Fund

Correspondent	The Administrator PO Box 1 Rosendale Lancashire BB4 5AB
CC No	1010204
Income	No information given
Grants	£7,655 (1997/98)
Trustees	The Trust operates anonymously
Area	North of England, Wales, Scotland and Ireland
Meets	January and July

Policy
The Trust did not respond to requests for information therefore the entry is based on information previously held by FINE.

The Women's Trust Fund (WTF) aims to support: women who wish to train in specific healing skills and who are not adequately funded to do this; women who need some help to start up in practice; groups setting up new projects to promote and campaign for women's health and well-being.

There is also a small emergency fund which provides assistance to existing projects in times of crisis on a one-off basis.

Individuals can apply to the WTF for up to £500 and groups can apply for up to £800. These grants are usually one-off and you do not need to be a registered charity to receive a grant.

The Women's Trust Fund (Cont..)

The WTF also offer start-up funding for groups / organisations such as Rape Crisis or health-related support groups.

Grants
All applications to the WTF are confidential, so no specific information has been provided. The guidelines give examples of what grants to women's health projects might be used for e.g. capital expenditure, publicity, telephone bills, postage, books.

Applications
Guidelines and application forms are available by writing to the Administrator. Completed applications need to be with the WTF by 1 January for consideration at the January meeting, or by 20 June for the July meeting.

The WTF does not acknowledge receipt of applications, but does inform all applicants of the outcome of their application, usually within 4 weeks of the meeting. Successful applicants should leave a year before reapplying.

Exclusions
The WTF **does not** fund:
- Anyone applying for their own health needs
- Anyone who seems to be adequately funded already
- People setting out to do a course for which they seem unlikely to raise the additional money needed beyond the WTF grant
- Anyone applying on behalf of another person or group
- Anyone aiming to do a course overseas, where there is a local equivalent
- Anyone applying for assistance to do a mainstream course leading to a widely recognised qualification, such as Nursing or Social Work

- Large charities with their own fundraising powers
- Organisations such as "Out of School Hours" clubs, nurseries or playgroups.

Yapp Charitable Trust

Correspondent   Margaret Thompson
47a Paris Road
Scholes
Holmfirth
HD9 1SY

Telephone   01484 683 403

Fax   01484 683 403

E-mail
yapp.trust@care4free.net

Website
www.yappcharitabletrust.org.uk

CC No   1076803

Income   £319,227 (2001)

Grants   £299,051 (2001)

Trustees   Rev. T C Brooke, Miss A J Norman, P Williams, P Murray, P R Davies

Area   UK

Meets   Three times a year, March, July and November

Policy

The Trust's policy is as follows:
- Elderly people
- Children and young people
- People with disabilities or mental health problems
- People trying to overcome life-limiting problems such as: addiction, relationship difficulties, abuse, a history of offending.

Grants are also made to support charities which work in the fields of:
- Education and learning (including lifelong learning)
- Scientific and medical research
- The Trust gives grants to small UK registered charities which have an annual turnover of less than £75,000. Grants range from £800 to £12,000 with the majority of grants being around £2,000. Most grants are for one year but applications for up to three years will be considered. Ongoing grants are rarely more than £3,000 a year.
- The Trust particularly wishes to encourage applications from charities working with elderly people. Although it no longer prioritises the North East, applications are still welcome.

Grants

Between 1999 / 2001 the Trust made 22 grants to charities in the North East, totalling £39,124.
- Trimdon Grange Youth Club - £500
- Northern Initiative on Women and Eating – £2,845
- Arthritis Care, Gateshead - £1,000
- Newcastle Jellicoe Sea Cadets - £1,500
- Hartlepool Special Needs Support Group - £2,000.

Applications

Applicants need to complete a simple form, available from the administrator at the address shown, and return it with supporting documents, such as annual accounts, annual reports and any pertinent leaflets.

Application forms and guidelines are available by e-mail in Word format and large print.

For summer holiday projects applications must be received in time for the November or March meetings. All applications need to be returned by: 31st January (March), 30th May (July), 30th September (November).

Yapp Charitable Trust (Cont..)

Previous successful applicants must wait three years before applying for another grant.

Unsuccessful applicants must wait for one year before applying again.

Exclusions

The Trustees **do not** make grants to applicants who fall into the following categories:
- Individuals
- Groups that do not have their own charity registration number or exemption
- Fundraising groups raising money to benefit another organisation, such as a hospital or a school.

The under-mentioned exclusions have also been introduced, but will be kept under review: (up to date details are available on the website)
- Work with under 5s
- Childcare
- Holidays and holiday centres
- Core funding of general community facilities such as community centres and village halls
- Capital expenditure – buildings, renovations, extensions, furnishings, equipment, minibuses.

York Diocese Social Care Fund

Correspondent	Veronica Lady Piercy Chairperson Fair View House Marton Sinnington York YO62 6RD
Telephone	01751 431976
CC No	1070900
Income	£6,736 (2001)
Grants	£9,513 (2001)
Trustees	Father A Campbell-Wilson, A Dorton, J Goodrich, Mrs H Fairwood, P Jefford CBE, Rt. Revd R S Ladds, A C Longthorp, Dr F Molyneux, V L Piercy, D W Taylor, Mrs R Usher
Area	Diocese of York only Middlesbrough, North York Moors, York, Selby, Hull
Meets	Quarterly

Policy

The Fund's object is to distribute funds contributed from parishes in the Diocese to groups and organisation within the area of the Diocese, which are setting up or running projects which aim to benefit the community.

These will be groups of people which are providing services, often on the basis of self or mutual help.

York Diocese Social Care Fund (Cont..)

Usually modest one-off grants are made to projects, but sometimes a larger grant can be made.

Grants
FINE has a full list of grants awarded. Groups and organisations that have been awarded grants have been church, children/parent, luncheon clubs etc.

Applications
Must be on an application form, which can be obtained from the correspondent along with the guidelines.

Exclusions
No individuals.

Yorkshire Agricultural Society

Correspondent	R T Keigwin Chief Executive Great Yorkshire Showground Harrogate HG2 8PW
Telephone	01423 541000
Fax	01423 541414
Email	info@yas.co.uk
Website	www.yas.co.uk
CC No	513238
Income	£2,802.349 (2001)
Grants	£122,218
Trustees	No information given
Area	North East England, Yorkshire and Humberside
Meets	Quarterly

Policy
The Trust did not respond to requests for information therefore the entry is based upon FINE research.

Aid to Agriculture
Under this programme support is available for research, education and environmental matters, within the context of farming.

An allocation from this budget is also made each year for applications from Universities and other institutions of higher education for small research grants to support research relevant to agriculture or the rural environment in the North East of England.

Yorkshire Agricultural Society (Cont..)

Grants
During 2000 grants awarded ranged from £200 to £7,500:
- £7,500 was made to Northumberland Durham Machinery Ring
- £500 was made for fruit tree planting in schools.

Applications
In writing to the correspondent. Letter to include a copy of accounts and proposed budget.

Applications should be:
- Timely and applied in nature
- Show originality
- Be of scientific merit
- Be relevant to North East England.

Exclusions
The Trust **does not** award grants for the following:
- Grants are not given for students fees or overseas projects
- Salaries and labour costs
- Expeditions
- Attendance at conferences
- Overheads
- Purchase or maintenance of equipment.

Yorkshire Bank Charitable Trust

Correspondent	Nicola Ashcroft Secretary to the Trustees 20 Merrion Way Leeds LS2 6NZ
CC No	326269
Income	No information available
Grants	No information available
Trustees	Graham Savage, Paul Fegen, John Hurst
Area	Within the area covered by the branches of the Bank (i.e. in England, from north of the Thames Valley to Newcastle upon Tyne)
Meets	Trustees meet every six / eight weeks. As a result responses to applicants can take time.

Policy
The Trust provides one-off grants for a specific project or part of a project, to registered charities only.

Charities which are considered for support include:
- Those engaged in Youth Work
- Facilities for the less able-bodied and mentally handicapped
- Counselling and community work in depressed areas

Yorkshire Bank Charitable Trust (Cont..)

- Some support for the arts and education.

The Trustees are unlikely to make more than one donation to an organisation within any 12 month period.

Grants
No information supplied.

Applications
Apply in writing to the correspondent. Applications can be submitted at any time and should include relevant details of the need the intended project is designed to meet.

Exclusions
The Trust **does not** support:
- Individuals, including students
- General appeals from national organisations.

Helpful Hint...

Plan properly before you contact funders. You need to be clear about what you want to do and plan your activities a year or two in advance to allow you time to raise money.

Subject Index

Exclusive Charity Haggerston Owners (ECHO)
The Esmee Fairbairn Foundation
Maurice Fry Charitable Trust
Greggs Trust
Hadrian Trust
Bill & May Hodgson Charitable Trust
The Joicey Trust
The Rose Joicey Fund
The Sir James Knott Trust
The Lankelly Foundation
The William Leech Charity
Lloyds TSB Foundation for England and Wales
The Sir Stephen Middleton Charity Trust
The Northern Rock Foundation
The Ropner Trust
The Rothley Trust
Christopher Rowbotham Charitable Trust
The Sedgefield Charities
Sherburn House Charity
The Bernard Sunley Charitable Foundation
The Tubney Charitable Trust
The Tyneside Charitable Trust
Garfield Weston Foundation
The 1989 Willan Charitable Trust
Yapp Charitable Trust
York Diocese Social Care Fund

Children / Young People

The Barbour Trust
BBC Children In Need
John Bell Charitable Trust
The Percy Bilton Charity
The J H Burn Charity Trust
Calouste Gulbenkian Foundation (UK Branch)
The Chase Charity
The Children's Foundation
Church Urban Fund
The De Clermont Charitable Company Limited
Cleveland Community Foundation
Comic Relief
Community Foundation serving Tyne & Wear and Northumberland
The Continuation Charitable Trust
Catherine Cookson Trust

County Durham Foundation
Hedley Denton Charitable Trust
Diana, Princess of Wales Memorial Fund
Dickon Trust
Exclusive Charity Haggerston Owners (ECHO)
The Esmee Fairbairn Foundation
The Four Winds Trust
Joseph Strong Frazer Trust
Maurice Fry Charitable Trust
The Goshen Trust
The Hospital of God at Greatham
Greggs Trust
Hadrian Trust
The W A Handley Charity Trust
Bill & May Hodgson Charitable Trust
The Ruth and Lionel Jacobson Charitable Trust
The Rose Joicey Fund
The Joicey Trust
The Sir James Knott Trust
The Lankelly Foundation
The William Leech Charity
Lloyds TSB Foundation for England and Wales
R W Mann Trustees Limited
Leslie and Lillian Manning Trust
The Sir Stephen Middleton Charity Trust
Northern Electric Employees Charity Association
The Northern Rock Foundation
Northumberland Foundation for Young People
Northumberland Rugby Union Charitable Trust
Northumberland Village Homes Trust
The Rank Foundation
The Ragdoll Foundation
The Ravenscroft Foundation
The Ropner Trust
The Ropner Centenary Trust
The Rothley Trust
Christopher Rowbotham Charitable Trust
Rural Youth Trust
St Hilda's Trust
Storrow Scott Charitable Will Trust
Sherburn House Charity
The Henry Smith Charity

The Bernard Sunley Charitable Foundation
Teesside Emergency Relief Fund
The TFM Cash Challenge Appeal
The Baily Thomas Charitable Fund
The Tubney Charitable Trust
Tyneside Charitable Trust
The Washington Community Development Trust
The Weavers' Company Benevolent Fund
The William Webster Charitable Trust
Garfield Weston Foundation
The 1989 Willan Charitable Trust
Yapp Charitable Trust
York Diocese Social Care Fund
Yorkshire Bank Charitable Trust

Community Care
Abbey National Charitable Trust
Ayton Charitable Trust
The Barbour Trust
The Percy Bilton Charity
The Chase Charity
Cleveland Community Foundation
The Continuation Charitable Trust
County Durham Foundation
Hedley Denton Charitable Trust
Exclusive Charity Haggerston Owners (ECHO)
The Esmee Fairbairn Foundation
The Hospital of God at Greatham
Hadrian Trust
The Ruth and Lionel Jacobson Charitable Trust
The Joicey Trust
The Sir James Knott Trust
The Lankelly Foundation
The William Leech Charity
Lloyds TSB Foundation for England and Wales
The Mahila Fund
R W Mann Trustees Limited
The Sir Stephen Middleton Charity Trust
Northern Electric Employees Charity Association
The Northern Rock Foundation
The Ropner Trust
The Rothley Trust

Christopher Rowbotham Charitable Trust
The Sedgefield Charities
Sherburn House Charity
The Henry Smith Charity
The Bernard Sunley Charitable Foundation
The TFM Cash Challenge Appeal
The Baily Thomas Charitable Fund
The Tubney Charitable Trust
The Tyneside Charitable Trust
Garfield Weston Foundation
The 1989 Willan Charitable Trust
Yapp Charitable Trust
York Diocese Social Care Fund

Community Development
The Barbour Trust
The Baring Foundation
The Percy Bilton Charity
Calouste Gulbenkian Foundation (UK Branch)
The Chase Charity
Church Urban Fund
Cleveland Community Foundation
Coalfields Regeneration Trust
Community Foundation serving Tyne & Wear and Northumberland
The Continuation Charitable Trust
County Durham Foundation
Exclusive Charity Haggerston Owners (ECHO)
The Esmee Fairbairn Foundation
J. Paul Getty Jr. General Charitable Trust
The Hospital of God at Greatham
Greggs Trust
Hadrian Trust
Hanson Environment Fund
The Joicey Trust
The Sir James Knott Trust
The Allen Lane Foundation
The Lankelly Foundation
The William Leech Charity
Lloyds TSB Foundation for England and Wales
R W Mann Trustees Limited
The Sir Stephen Middleton Charity Trust
Northern Electric Employees Charity Association

The Northern Rock Foundation
The Ravenscroft Foundation
The Ropner Trust
The Rothley Trust
Christopher Rowbotham Charitable Trust
Storrow Scott Charitable Will Trust
The Sedgefield Charities
Shears Charitable Trust
Sherburn House Charity
SITA Environmental Trust
The Bernard Sunley Charitable Foundation
The Washington Community Development Trust
Garfield Weston Foundation
The 1989 Willan Charitable Trust
York Diocese Social Care Fund
Yorkshire Bank Charitable Trust

Conservation of Buildings (including Churches)

The Barbour Trust
The J H Burn Charity Trust
The Chase Charity
The De Clermont Charitable Company Limited
The Continuation Charitable Trust
Catherine Cookson Trust
County Durham Foundation
Lord Crewe's Charity
Hedley Denton Charitable Trust
The Esmee Fairbairn Charitable Trust
J. Paul Getty Jr. General Charitable Trust
Hadrian Trust
The W A Handley Charity Trust
Bill & May Hodgson Charitable Trust
The Sir James Knott Trust
The Sir Stephen Middleton Charity Trust
Northumbria Historic Churches Trust
Sir John Priestman Charity Trust
The Ropner Trust
Shears Environmental Trust
SITA Environmental Trust
The Bernard Sunley Charitable Foundation
Thompson's of Prudhoe Environmental Trust
The Tubney Charitable Trust

Garfield Weston Foundation

Counselling

The Camelot Foundation
The Children's Foundation
The De Clermont Charitable Company Limited
Cleveland Community Foundation
The Continuation Charitable Trust
County Durham Foundation
Exclusive Charity Haggerston Owners (ECHO)
Maurice Fry Charitable Trust
J. Paul Getty Jr. General Charitable Trust
The Hospital of God at Greatham
Greggs Trust
Hadrian Trust
Bill & May Hodgson Charitable Trust
The Joicey Trust
The Sir James Knott Trust
The Allen Lane Foundation
The William Leech Charity
Lloyds TSB Foundation for England and Wales
R W Mann Trustees Limited
The Sir Stephen Middleton Charity Trust
Northern Electric Employees Charity Association
Northumberland Village Homes Trust
The Ropner Trust
The Ropner Centenary Trust
The Rothley Trust
Sherburn House Charity
The Henry Smith Charity
The Bernard Sunley Charitable Foundation
The Tubney Charitable Trust
The Tudor Trust
The William Webster Charitable Trust
Garfield Weston Foundation
The 1989 Willan Charitable Trust
Yapp Charitable Trust
York Diocese Social Care Fund
Yorkshire Bank Charitable Trust

People with Disabilities

Abbey National Charitable Trust
The Ayton Charitable Trust
The Barbour Trust

The Percy Bilton Charity
Calouste Gulbenkian Foundation (UK Branch)
The Camelot Foundation
The Chase Charity
The Children's Foundation
The De Clermont Charitable Company Limited
Cleveland Community Foundation
Comic Relief
Community Foundation serving Tyne & Wear
The Continuation Charitable Trust
Catherine Cookson Trust
County Durham Foundation
Hedley Denton Charitable Trust
Exclusive Charity Haggerston Owners (ECHO)
The Esmee Fairbairn Foundation
Joseph Strong Frazer Trust
The Hospital of God at Greatham
Greggs Trust
Hadrian Trust
The W A Handley Charity Trust
The Ruth and Lionel Jacobson Charitable Trust
The Joicey Trust
The Rose Joicey Fund
The Sir James Knott Trust
Lankelly Foundation
The William Leech Charity
Lloyds TSB Foundation for England and Wales
R W Mann Trustees Limited
Leslie and Lillian Manning Trust
The Sir Stephen Middleton Charity Trust
Northern Electric Employees Charity Association
The Northern Rock Foundation
Northumberland Foundation for Young People
The Rank Foundation
The Ravenscroft Foundation
The Ropner Trust
The Ropner Centenary Trust
The Rothley Trust
Christopher Rowbotham Charitable Trust
The Royal Victoria Trust for the Blind
The Sedgefield Charities

Shears Charitable Trust
Sherburn House Charity
The Henry Smith Charity
The Bernard Sunley Charitable Foundation
Teesside Emergency Relief Fund
The TFM Cash Challenge Appeal
The Baily Thomas Charitable Fund
The Tubney Charitable Trust
The Tyneside Charitable Trust
The William Webster Charitable Trust
Garfield Weston Foundation
The 1989 Willan Charitable Trust
Yapp Charitable Trust
York Diocese Social Care Fund
Yorkshire Bank Charitable Trust

Disadvantaged / Poverty
Abbey National Charitable Trust
The Ayton Charitable Trust
The Barbour Trust
The Percy Bilton Charity
Calouste Gulbenkian Foundation (UK Branch)
The Children's Foundation
Church Urban Fund
Cleveland Community Foundation
Comic Relief
Community Foundation serving Tyne & Wear and Northumberland
The Continuation Charitable Trust
County Durham Foundation
Hedley Denton Charitable Trust
The Esmee Fairbairn Charitable Trust
The Four Winds Trust
Maurice Fry Charitable Trust
J. Paul Getty Jr. General Charitable Trust
The Hospital of God at Greatham
Greggs Trust
Hadrian Trust
Bill & May Hodgson Charitable Trust
The Ruth and Lionel Jacobson Charitable Trust
The Rose Joicey Fund
The Sir James Knott Trust
The Lankelly Foundation
The William Leech Charity
Lloyds TSB Foundation for England and Wales
R W Mann Trustees Limited

The Sir Stephen Middleton Charity Trust
The Northern Rock Foundation
Northumberland Foundation for Young People
Northumberland Village Homes Trust
The Ravenscroft Foundation
The Ropner Trust
The Ropner Centenary Trust
The Rothley Trust
Christopher Rowbotham Charitable Trust
The St Hilda's Trust
The Sedgefield Charities
Shears Charitable Trust
Sherburn House Charity
The Henry Smith Charity
The Bernard Sunley Charitable Foundation
Teesside Emergency Relief Fund
The TFM Cash Challenge Appeal
The Wallsend Charitable Trust
The William Webster Charitable Trust
Garfield Weston Foundation
The 1989 Willan Charitable Trust
Yapp Charitable Trust
York Diocese Social Care Fund

Education / Training
Abbey National Charitable Trust
The Baring Foundation
The Percy Bilton Charity
Calouste Gulbenkian Foundation (UK Branch)
The Camelot Foundation
The Children's Foundation
Cleveland Community Foundation
Coalfields Regeneration Trust
Community Foundation serving Tyne & Wear and Northumberland
The Continuation Charitable Trust
Catherine Cookson Trust
County Durham Foundation
Hedley Denton Charitable Trust
The Esmee Fairbairn Foundation
Joseph Strong Frazer Trust
Hadrian Trust
The W A Handley Charity Trust
The Joicey Trust
The Sir James Knott Trust

Lloyds TSB Foundation for England and Wales
The Mahila Fund
R W Mann Trustees Limited
The Sir Stephen Middleton Charity Trust
Northumberland Foundation for Young People
Northumberland Village Homes Trust
The Rank Foundation
The Ropner Trust
The Ropner Centenary Trust
The Rothley Trust
Christopher Rowbotham Charitable Trust
The Royal Victoria Trust for the Blind
Rural Youth Trust
Storrow Scott Charitable Will Trust
The Sedgefield Charities
Shears Charitable Trust
The Shaftoe Educational Trust
Sherburn House Charity
The Bernard Sunley Charitable Foundation
The TFM Cash Challenge Appeal
The Tubney Charitable Trust
The Vardy Foundation
The William Webster Charitable Trust
Garfield Weston Foundation
The 1989 Willan Charitable Trust
Yapp Charitable Trust
York Diocese Social Care Fund
Yorkshire Agricultural Society
Yorkshire Bank Charitable Trust

Employment Training / Unemployed
Abbey National Charitable Trust
The Barbour Trust
Percy Bilton Charity
The Camelot Foundation
Cleveland Community Foundation
Coalfields Regeneration Trust
Community Foundation serving Tyne & Wear and Northumberland
The Continuation Charitable Trust
County Durham Foundation
Hedley Denton Charitable Trust
The Esmee Fairbairn Foundation
J. Paul Getty Jr. General Charitable Trust

Greggs Trust
Hadrian Trust
The Rose Joicey Fund
The Joicey Trust
The Sir James Knott Trust
The Allen Lane Foundation
The William Leech Charity
Lloyds TSB Foundation for England and Wales
The Sir Stephen Middleton Charity Trust
The Northern Rock Foundation
The Ropner Trust
The Rothley Trust
Christopher Rowbotham Charitable Trust
Rural Youth Trust
Shears Charitable Trust
Sherburn House Charity
The Bernard Sunley Charitable Foundation
The Baily Thomas Charitable Fund
The William Webster Charitable Trust
Garfield Weston Foundation
The 1989 Willan Charitable Trust
Yapp Charitable Trust

Environment / Nature Conservation
The Barbour Trust
John Bell Charitable Trust
The De Clermont Charitable Company Limited
CDENT Environment and Waste Fund
Coalfields Regeneration Trust
Community Foundation serving Tyne & Wear and Northumberland
The Continuation Charitable Trust
Catherine Cookson Trust
County Durham Foundation
Hedley Denton Charitable Trust
The Esmee Fairbairn Foundation
The Four Winds Trust
J. Paul Getty Jr. General Charitable Trust
Hadrian Trust
Hanson Environmental Fund
Bill & May Hodgson Charitable Trust
The Sir James Knott Trust
R W Mann Trustees Limited

The Sir Stephen Middleton Charity Trust
The Northern Rock Foundation
The Ropner Trust
Christopher Rowbotham Charitable Trust
Rural Youth Trust
Shears Charitable Trust
SITA Environmental Trust
The Bernard Sunley Charitable Foundation
Thompson's of Prudhoe Environmental Trust
The Tubney Charitable Trust
Garfield Weston Foundation
The 1989 Willan Charitable Trust
Yorkshire Agricultural Society

Ethnic Minority / Race Relations
Charities Aid Foundation
Cleveland Community Foundation
Community Foundation serving Tyne & Wear and Northumberland
The Continuation Charitable Trust
County Durham Foundation
Diana, Princess of Wales Memorial Trust
The Esmee Fairbairn Foundation
J. Paul Getty Jr. General Charitable Trust
Greggs Trust
Hadrian Trust
The Joicey Trust
The Rose Joicey Fund
The Sir James Knott Trust
The Allen Lane Foundation
The Lankelly Foundation
The William Leech Charity
Lloyds TSB Foundation for England and Wales
The Sir Stephen Middleton Charity Trust
The Northern Rock Foundation
The Ropner Trust
The Rothley Trust
The Bernard Sunley Charitable Foundation
Garfield Weston Foundation
The 1989 Willan Charitable Trust
The Women's Trust Fund

Ex-Offenders / Offenders
The Ayton Charitable Trust
The Chase Charity
The Continuation Charitable Trust
County Durham Foundation
Diana, Princess of Wales Memorial Fund
The Esmee Fairbairn Foundation
J. Paul Getty Jr. General Charitable Trust
The Hospital of God at Greatham
Greggs Trust
Hadrian Trust
The Rose Joicey Fund
The Sir James Knott Trust
The Allen Lane Foundation
The Lankelly Foundation
The William Leech Charity
Lloyds TSB Foundation for England and Wales
R W Mann Trustees Limited
The Sir Stephen Middleton Charity Trust
The Ropner Trust
The Rothley Trust
The Bernard Sunley Charitable Foundation
The Tudor Trust
The Weavers' Company Benevolent Fund
The William Webster Charitable Trust
Garfield Weston Foundation
The 1989 Willan Charitable Trust
Yapp Charitable Trust
York Diocese Social Care Fund

Family Life / Welfare
The Barbour Trust
John Bell Charitable Trust
Calouste Gulbenkian Foundation (UK Branch)
The Chase Charity
Children's Foundation
Church Urban Fund
Cleveland Community Foundation
Community Foundation serving Tyne & Wear and Northumberland
The Continuation Charitable Trust
County Durham Foundation
Exclusive Charity Haggerston Owners (ECHO)

The Esmee Fairbairn Foundation
J. Paul Getty Jr. General Charitable Trust
The Hospital of God at Greatham
Greggs Trust
Hadrian Trust
The Joicey Trust
The Rose Joicey Fund
The Sir James Knott Trust
The Lankelly Foundation
The William Leech Charity
Lloyds TSB Foundation for England and Wales
R W Mann Trustees Limited
The Sir Stephen Middleton Charity Trust
Northern Electric Employees Charity Association
The Northern Rock Foundation
Northumberland Foundation for Young People
The Ropner Trust
The Rothley Trust
Christopher Rowbotham Charitable Trust
The Sedgefield Charities
Sherburn House Charity
The Henry Smith Charity
The Bernard Sunley Charitable Foundation
Teesside Emergency Relief Fund
The TFM Cash Challenge Appeal
The Tudor Trust
Garfield Weston Foundation
The 1989 Willan Charitable Trust
Yapp Charitable Trust
York Diocese Social Care Fund

General Charitable Purposes
Ayton Charitable Trust
The Barbour Trust
John Bell Charitable Trust
The Benfield Motors Charitable Trust
J H Burn Charity Trust
Calouste Gulbenkian Foundation (UK Branch)
The Century Radio Limited Charitable Trust
The J H Burn Charity Trust
The De Clermont Charitable Company Limited

Cleveland Community Foundation
The Continuation Charitable Trust
Catherine Cookson Trust
County Durham Foundation
Lord Crewe's Charity
Cumberland Building Society
Charitable Foundation
Hedley Denton Charitable Trust
Dickon Trust
Exclusive Charity Haggerston Owners (ECHO)
Joseph Strong Frazer Trust
The Goshen Trust
The W A Handley Charity Trust
John Haswell Memorial Trust
Bill & May Hodgson Charitable Trust
The Ruth and Lionel Jacobson Charitable Trust
The Joicey Trust
The Kelly Charitable Trust
The Sir James Knott Trust
The William Leech Charity
Lloyds TSB Foundation for England and Wales
R W Mann Trustees Limited
Leslie and Lillian Manning Trust
The Sir Stephen Middleton Charity Trust
Northern Electric Employees Charity Association
Northumberland Foundation for Young People
Sir John Priestman Charity Trust
The Rank Foundation
The Ravenscroft Foundation
The Ropner Trust
The Ropner Centenary Trust
The Rothley Trust
Christopher Rowbotham Charitable Trust
The Storrow Scott Charitable Will Trust
The Smith (Haltwhistle) Charitable Trust
The Bernard Sunley Charitable Foundation
Teesside Emergency Relief Fund
The TFM Cash Challenge Appeal
Tyneside Charitable Trust
The Washington Community Development Trust
The William Webster Charitable Trust

Garfield Weston Foundation
The 1989 Willan Charitable Trust
York Diocese Social Care Fund

Health / Medicine
The Ayton Charitable Trust
The Barbour Trust
John Bell Charitable Trust
Benfield Motors Charitable Trust
J H Burn Charitable Trust
Calouste Gulbenkian Foundation (UK Branch)
The Children's Foundation
The De Clermont Charitable Company Limited
Community Foundation serving Tyne & Wear and Northumberland
The Continuation Charitable Trust
Catherine Cookson Trust
Hedley Denton Charitable Trust
Exclusive Charity Haggerston Owners (ECHO)
Joseph Strong Frazer Trust
The W A Handley Charity Trust
Bill & May Hodgson Charitable Trust
The Ruth and Lionel Jacobson Charitable Trust
The Sir James Knott Trust
The William Leech Charity
Lloyds TSB Foundation for England and Wales
The Mahila Fund
R W Mann Trustees Limited
Leslie and Lillian Manning Trust
The Sir Stephen Middleton Charity Trust
Northern Electric Employees Charity Association
Northumberland Village Homes Trust
The Ropner Trust
The Ropner Centenary Trust
The Rothley Trust
Christopher Rowbotham Charitable Trust
Storrow Scott Charitable Will Trust
The Sedgefield Charities
Shears Charitable Trust
Sherburn House Charity
The Henry Smith Charity

The Bernard Sunley Charitable Foundation
The Tudor Trust
The Tubney Charitable Trust
The Tyneside Charitable Trust
The Vardy Foundation
The William Webster Charitable Trust
Garfield Weston Foundation
The 1989 Willan Charitable Trust
The Women's Trust Fund
Yapp Charitable Trust

Homeless / Housing
The Ayton Charitable Trust
The Barbour Trust
The Chase Charity
Church Urban Fund
Cleveland Community Foundation
Community Foundation serving Tyne & Wear and Northumberland
The Continuation Charitable Trust
County Durham Foundation
Hedley Denton Charitable Trust
The Esmee Fairbairn Foundation
J. Paul Getty Jr. General Charitable Trust
The Hospital of God at Greatham
Greggs Trust
Hadrian Trust
The W A Handley Charity Trust
Bill & May Hodgson Charitable Trust
The Ruth and Lionel Jacobson Charitable Trust
The Joicey Trust
The Rose Joicey Fund
The Sir James Knott Trust
The Lankelly Foundation
The William Leech Charity
Lloyds TSB Foundation for England and Wales
R W Mann Trustees Limited
Leslie and Lillian Manning Trust
The Sir Stephen Middleton Charity Trust
The Ropner Trust
The Rothley Trust
Sherburn House Charity
The Henry Smith Charity
The Bernard Sunley Charitable Foundation
The Tudor Trust

The Wallsend Charitable Trust
The William Webster Charitable Trust
Garfield Weston Foundation
The 1989 Willan Charitable Trust
Yapp Charitable Trust
York Diocese Social Care Fund

Hospices / Hospitals
The Ayton Charitable Trust
The Barbour Trust
John Bell Charitable Trust
Benfield Motors Charitable Trust
The J H Burn Charity Trust
Cleveland Community Foundation
The Continuation Charitable Trust
County Durham Foundation
Hedley Denton Charitable Trust
Exclusive Charity Haggerston Owners (ECHO)
Joseph Strong Frazer Trust
The Goshen Trust
Greggs Trust
Hadrian Trust
The W A Handley Charity Trust
Bill & May Hodgson Charitable Trust
The Ruth and Lionel Jacobson Charitable Trust
The Rose Joicey Fund
The Joicey Trust
The Sir James Knott Trust
The William Leech Charity
Lloyds TSB Foundation for England and Wales
R W Mann Trustees Limited
Leslie and Lillian Manning Trust
The Sir Stephen Middleton Charity Trust
Northern Electric Employees Charity Association
The Ropner Trust
The Rothley Trust
Christopher Rowbotham Charitable Trust
Sherburn House Charity
The Henry Smith Charity
The Bernard Sunley Charitable Foundation
Teesside Emergency Relief Fund
The TFM Cash Challenge Appeal
The Tubney Charitable Trust
The Tyneside Charitable Trust

Garfield Weston Foundation
The 1989 Willan Charitable Trust
Yapp Charitable Trust
York Diocese Social Care Fund

International
The Baring Foundation
The De Clermont Charitable Company Limited
Comic Relief
The Continuation Charitable Trust
Hedley Denton Charitable Trust
The Goshen Trust
Bill & May Hodgson Charitable Trust
The William Leech Charity
The Rothley Trust
The Bernard Sunley Charitable Foundation
The 1989 Willan Charitable Trust

Mental Health
The Ayton Charitable Trust
The Barbour Trust
The Percy Bilton Charity
The Camelot Foundation
The Chase Charity
The Children's Foundation
The De Clermont Charitable Company Limited
Cleveland Community Foundation
Comic Relief
The Continuation Charitable Trust
County Durham Foundation
Hedley Denton Charitable Trust
Diana, Princess of Wales Memorial Trust
Exclusive Charity Haggerston Owners (ECHO)
The Esmee Fairbairn Foundation
J. Paul Getty Jr. General Charitable Trust
The Hospital of God at Greatham
Greggs Trust
Hadrian Trust
Bill & May Hodgson Charitable Trust
The Ruth and Lionel Jacobson Charitable Trust
The Rose Joicey Fund
The Joicey Trust
The Sir James Knott Trust
The Allen Lane Foundation

The Lankelly Foundation
The William Leech Charity
Lloyds TSB Foundation for England and Wales
R W Mann Trustees Limited
Leslie and Lillian Manning Trust
The Sir Stephen Middleton Charity Trust
Northern Electric Employees Charity Association
The Northern Rock Foundation
The Ropner Trust
The Rothley Trust
Christopher Rowbotham Charitable Trust
Sherburn House Charity
The Henry Smith Charity
The Bernard Sunley Charitable Foundation
The TFM Cash Challenge Appeal
The Tubney Charitable Trust
The Tudor Trust
The Tyneside Charitable Trust
The William Webster Charitable Trust
Garfield Weston Foundation
The 1989 Willan Charitable Trust
The Women's Trust Fund
Yapp Charitable Trust
York Diocese Social Care Fund

Older People
The Ayton Charitable Trust
The Barbour Trust
John Bell Charitable Trust
Benfield Motors Charitable Trust
The Percy Bilton Charity
The Chase Charity
The De Clermont Charitable Company Limited
Cleveland Community Foundation
The Continuation Charitable Trust
Catherine Cookson Trust
County Durham Foundation
Hedley Denton Charitable Trust
Exclusive Charity Haggerston Owners (ECHO)
The Esmee Fairbairn Foundation
Joseph Strong Frazer Trust
The Hospital of God at Greatham
Greggs Trust
Hadrian Trust

The W A Handley Charity Trust
Bill & May Hodgson Charitable Trust
The Rose Joicey Fund
The Joicey Trust
The Sir James Knott Trust
The Allen Lane Foundation
The Lankelly Foundation
The William Leech Charity
Lloyds TSB Foundation for England and Wales
R W Mann Trustees Limited
Leslie and Lillian Manning Trust
The Sir Stephen Middleton Charity Trust
Northern Electric Employees Charity Association
The Northern Rock Foundation
The Rank Foundation
The Ropner Trust
Christopher Rowbotham Charitable Trust
The Sedgefield Charities
Sherburn House Charity
The Henry Smith Charity
The Bernard Sunley Charitable Foundation
Teesside Emergency Relief Fund
The Tudor Trust
The Tyneside Charitable Trust
The Wallsend Charitable Trust
The William Webster Charitable Trust
Garfield Weston Foundation
The 1989 Willan Charitable Trust
Yapp Charitable Trust
York Diocese Social Care Fund

Recreation / Leisure / Sport
Percy Bilton Charity
The Children's Foundation
Cleveland Community Foundation
Community Foundation serving Tyne & Wear and Northumberland
The Continuation Charitable Trust
County Durham Foundation
Exclusive Charity Haggerston Owners (ECHO)
The Foundation for Sport and the Arts
Joseph Strong Frazer Trust
Hanson Environment Fund
The Rose Joicey Fund
The Sir James Knott Trust

Lloyds TSB Foundation for England and Wales
R W Mann Trustees Limited
The Sir Stephen Middleton Charity Trust
The Northern Rock Foundation
Northumberland Rugby Union Charitable Trust
The Ropner Trust
The Rothley Trust
Christopher Rowbotham Charitable Trust
The Sedgefield Charities
The Bernard Sunley Charitable Foundation
The TFM Cash Challenge Appeal
Thompson's of Prudhoe Environmental Trust
The Tudor Trust
The Washington Community Development Trust
The William Webster Charitable Trust
Garfield Weston Foundation
The 1989 Willan Charitable Trust

Religious Activities
Benfield Motors Charitable Trust
Goshen Trust
W A Handley Charity Trust
The Rank Foundation
The Vardy Foundation
Garfield Weston Foundation

Research
Catherine Cookson Trust
The Allen Lane Foundation
The Northern Rock Foundation
The Henry Smith Charity
The Baily Thomas Charitable Trust
Yorkshire Agricultural Society

Social Welfare
The Barbour Trust
John Bell Charitable Trust
Benfield Motors Charitable Trust
The Chase Charity
The Children's Foundation
Church Urban Fund
Cleveland Community Foundation
Coalfields Regeneration Trust

Community Foundation serving Tyne & Wear and Northumberland
The Continuation Charitable Trust
County Durham Foundation
Exclusive Charity Haggerston Owners (ECHO)
The Esmee Fairbairn Foundation
J. Paul Getty Jr. General Charitable Trust
The Hospital of God at Greatham
Greggs Trust
Hadrian Trust
The W A Handley Charity Trust
The Rose Joicey Fund
The Joicey Trust
The Sir James Knott Trust
The Allen Lane Foundation
The Lankelly Foundation
The William Leech Charity
Lloyds TSB Foundation for England and Wales
R W Mann Trustees Limited
Leslie and Lilian Manning Trust
The Sir Stephen Middleton Charity Trust
Northern Electric Employees Charity Association
The Northern Rock Foundation
The Ropner Trust
The Ropner Centenary Trust
The Rothley Trust
Christopher Rowbotham Charitable Trust
Sedgefield Charities
Sherburn House Charity
The Bernard Sunley Charitable Foundation
Teesside Emergency Relief Fund
The TFM Cash Challenge Appeal
The Tudor Trust
The Wallsend Charitable Trust
The Weavers' Company Benevolent Fund
The William Webster Charitable Trust
Garfield Weston Foundation
The 1989 Willan Charitable Trust
York Diocese Social Care Fund

Women's Organisations
The Barbour Trust
The Percy Bilton Charity

Cleveland Community Foundation
Comic Relief
Community Foundation serving Tyne & Wear and Northumberland
The Continuation Charitable Trust
County Durham Foundation
Maurice Fry Charitable Trust
J. Paul Getty Jr. General Charitable Trust
Greggs Trust
Hadrian Trust
The Rose Joicey Fund
The Sir James Knott Trust
The Lankelly Foundation
The William Leech Charity
Lloyds TSB Foundation for England and Wales
The Mahila Fund
R W Mann Trustees Limited
The Sir Stephen Middleton Charity Trust
Northern Electric Employees Charity Association
The Northern Rock Foundation
The Ropner Trust
The Rothley Trust
The Bernard Sunley Charitable Foundation
The TFM Cash Challenge Appeal
Garfield Weston Foundation
The 1989 Willan Charitable Trust
The Women's Trust Fund
Yapp Charitable Trust
York Diocese Social Care Fund

Other Areas of Work
Campaigning
Millfield House Foundation

Maritime Charities / Service Charities
The J H Burn Charity Trust
De Clermont Charitable Company Limited
Joseph Strong Frazer Trust
The Sir James Knott Trust
The Ropner Centenary Trust
Bernard Sunley Charitable Foundation
Tyneside Charitable Trust

Policy Issues
Millfield House Foundation

Strengthening The Voluntary Sector
Charities Aid Foundation
Cleveland Community Foundation
Lloyds TSB Foundation for England and
Wales
The Northern Rock Foundation